South Africa

by Richard Whitaker

Richard Whitaker is a university professor of Classics in South Africa and a freelance travel writer who has travelled extensively in Southern Africa, Europe, Turkey, the USA and Australia. He has contributed to the AA's *Adventure Traveller Southern Africa* guide. This is his first guidebook for the Essential series.

Above: a female leopard at Tshukudu Game Reserve, Mpumalanga

AA Publishing

Above: *Pretoria's jacaranda trees in full bloom*

Written by Richard Whitaker

First published 2001
Reprinted May 2003
Reprinted 2004. Information verified and updated.
Reprinted Jul 2004
Reprinted April 2005

© Automobile Association Developments Limited 2004
Maps © Automobile Association Developments Limited 2003

Published by AA Publishing, a trading name of Automobile Association Developments Limited, whose registered office is Southwood East, Apollo Rise, Farnborough, Hampshire, GU14 0JW. Registered number 1878835.

Automobile Association Developments Limited retains the copyright in the original edition © 2001 and in all subsequent editions, reprints and amendments.

A CIP catalogue record for this book is available from the British Library.

All rights reserved. No part of this publication may be reproduced, stored in a retrieval system, or transmitted in any form or by any means – electronic, photocopying, recording or otherwise – unless the written permission of the publishers has been obtained beforehand. This book may not be sold, resold, hired out or otherwise disposed of by way of trade in any form of binding or cover other than that in which it is published, without the prior consent of the publisher.

The contents of this publication are believed correct at the time of printing. Nevertheless, AA Publishing accept no responsibility for errors, omissions or changes in the details given, or for the consequences of readers' reliance on this information. This does not affect your statutory rights. Assessments of attractions, hotels and restaurants are based upon the author's own experience and contain subjective opinions that may not reflect the publisher's opinion or a reader's experience. We have tried to ensure accuracy, but things do change, so please let us know if you have any comments or corrections.

Find out more about AA Publishing and the wide range of travel publications and services the AA provides by visiting our website at www.theAA.com

A02622

Colour separation: Chroma Graphics (Overseas) Pte Ltd, Singapore
Printed and bound in Italy by Printer Trento S.r.l.

Contents

About this Book

KEY TO SYMBOLS

🔡 map reference to the maps found in the What to See section

✉ address or location

☎ telephone number

🕐 opening times

🍴 restaurant or café on premises or near by

🚌 nearest bus/tram route

⛴ ferry crossings and boat excursions

✈ travel by air

ℹ tourist information

♿ facilities for visitors with disabilities

✋ admission charge

↔ other places of interest near by

❓ other practical information

➤ indicates the page where you will find a fuller description

This book is divided into five sections to cover the most important aspects of your visit to South Africa.

Viewing South Africa pages 5–14
An introduction to South Africa by the author.
South Africa's Features
Essence of South Africa
The Shaping of South Africa
Peace and Quiet
South Africa's Famous

Top Ten pages 15–26
The author's choice of the Top Ten places to see in South Africa, listed in alphabetical order, each with practical information.

What to See pages 27–90
The four main areas of South Africa, each with its own brief introduction and an alphabetical listing of the main attractions.
Practical information
Snippets of 'Did you know…' information
3 suggested walks
4 suggested tours
2 excursions
2 features

Where To… pages 91–116
Detailed listings of the best places to eat, stay, shop, take the children and be entertained.

Practical Matters pages 117–24
A highly visual section containing essential travel information.

Maps
All map references are to the individual maps found in the What to See section of this guide.
For example, Kruger National Park has the reference 🔡 54C4 – indicating the page on which the map is located and the grid square in which the national park is to be found. A list of the maps that have been used in this travel guide can be found in the index.

Prices
Where appropriate, an indication of the cost of an establishment is given by **£** signs:
£££ denotes higher prices, **££** denotes average prices, while **£** denotes lower charges.

Star Ratings
Most of the places described in this book have been given a separate rating:

😳😳😳 Do not miss
😳😳 Highly recommended
😳 Worth seeing

Viewing South Africa

Above:
African
masks make
ever-popular
souvenirs
Right: the
flag of the
'New'
South
Africa flying
proudly

Richard Whitaker's South Africa

Game Parks
Kruger National Park; Greater St Lucia Wetland; Addo Elephant National Park.

Landscapes
Table Mountain; the Drakensberg Mountains; the Karoo.

Coast and Beaches
Cape Town's Clifton Beach; Transkei Wild Coast; Natal South Coast.

Leisure and Nightlife
Victoria and Alfred Waterfront.

Below: *Table Mountain covered with a thick 'tablecloth' of cloud*
Inset: *a lilac-breasted roller sunbathing*

What the tourist brochures say about South Africa is true – this really is 'A World in One Country'. You can travel from the Western Cape with its Mediterranean climate, through arid semi-desert areas in the interior, through bushveld and savannah to the subtropical coast of KwaZulu-Natal. You can hike on Table Mountain or in the spectacular Drakensberg Mountains, and drive through the haunting, empty plains of the Karoo. Modern cities such as Cape Town, Johannesburg and Durban contrast with shanty towns and tiny country villages.

The people of this country are one of its greatest strengths. If you smile, acknowledge those you meet and take a minute or two to chat, you will normally encounter enormous friendliness and willingness to help. Remember, however, that many people in South Africa are desperately poor, there are still considerable social problems and crime is a concern – particularly in the inner cities.

For the tourist, South Africa offers many different types of holiday. Soak up the sun on the endless, almost deserted beaches of the Transkei Wild Coast. Go river-rafting, sea-kayaking or pluck up courage and do the world's highest bungee-jump from the Bloukrans River bridge. Or enjoy the theatres, cinemas, restaurants and nightclubs in the cities.

Lovers of wildlife can indulge themselves to the full, watching birds in the mountains, forests and wetlands, or going in search of the Big Five – lion, buffalo, elephant, rhino and leopard – in the country's outstanding National Parks.

South Africa is huge, beautiful, mountainous, flat, dry, humid, friendly, sometimes dangerous, but never boring.

South Africa's Features

Geography
- South Africa is a vast country, covering 1,221,000sq km, with nearly 3,000km of coastline.
- Its highest point is in the Drakensberg (3,410m).
- From the coast the land rises steeply to the large interior plateau, comprising most of the country.

Climate
- Apart from the Western Cape, which has a Mediterranean climate with winter rainfall, the rest of South Africa is a summer rainfall area.
- Average temperatures for the country range from 0–20°C in midwinter to 15–35°C in midsummer.

Languages
- South Africa has 11 official languages: Afrikaans, English, Ndebele, Northern Sotho, Southern Sotho, Si Swati, Tsonga, Tswana, Venda, Xhosa and Zulu.
- English is most commonly used for official purposes.

Economy
- The major sectors are mining, agriculture and fishing, manufacturing industries and, increasingly, tourism.

People
Archbishop Tutu has rightly called South Africa the 'Rainbow Nation'. The largest part of the 'rainbow' is the black African majority. Indigenous Bushmen (San) and Khoikhoi ('Hottentot'), Dutch settlers, Indonesians originally brought to the Cape as slaves, settlers from England and many other European countries, and immigrants from elsewhere in Africa, make up the rest of the spectrum.

Local Names
Many South African cities have a local African name as well as an official name that appears on the map. Johannesburg is also known as 'Egoli' ('place of gold'), Kimberley as 'Ndayimani' ('diamond'), Durban as 'eThegwini' ('place of the thekwane' – a kind of bird), Port Elizabeth as 'Ibayi' ('the Bay') and Cape Town as 'Khepi' ('Cape').

Below: *Venda people pose for the cameras*

Below: *South Africa's highest mountains, the Drakensberg*

Essence of South Africa

Below: *cream of tartar comes from the fruit of the baobab tree*
Main picture: *game-viewing in style at a private reserve*

The essence of South Africa lies in the resolve and courage of its people, in its landscapes, flora and fauna, in the edgy vibrancy of its cities. The open plains, the hot bushveld, the mountains and beaches, the baobab trees, the elephants and the lions, have always been there. But because of the willingness of South Africans to talk and compromise – which brought about the democratic transformation of 1994 – far more people than in the past can enjoy these now. At the same time, South Africa's cities are expanding rapidly – shiny new office blocks contrast with sprawling, dusty, shanty towns.

THE **10** ESSENTIALS

If you only have a short time to visit South Africa, or would like to get a really complete picture of the country, here are some of the essentials:

• **Take a trail through a national park**. Walk with a seasoned ranger, camp in the bush and see South Africa's wildlife up close.

• **Swim at Plettenberg Bay** from some of the most beautiful, golden beaches in the world (➤ 19).

• **Canoe or raft the Orange River** and experience the ultimate in peace and quiet. At night you will see more stars than you've ever seen before (➤ 114).

• **Visit a township** on an organised tour or with a resident you know. Created by apartheid for urban blacks, the townships are where the majority of South Africa's city-dwellers live.

• **Go down a gold mine**. Experience first hand what hundreds of thousands of men have gone through to produce the country's premier export.

• **Travel long-distance by train**. This is a wonderful way to take in the countryside while getting from one city to the next. You can ride in expensive luxury on the Blue Train or Rovos Rail, or cheaply on the ordinary trains.

• **Enjoy a *braai* (barbecue)**. South Africans love to cook out in the open air. Get to know the locals and you're almost certain to be invited to one.

• **Visit a wine farm** in the Western Cape, taste the wines (and the cheeses that many farms also produce) and enjoy a leisurely lunch under the oak trees (➤ 42).

• **Listen to music at a jazz club**. Some of the world's finest jazz musicians started out from the local clubs. Experience their vibrant atmosphere, and perhaps get a sneak preview of the next international star.

• **Buy local art**. South African art is a fascinating hybrid of African and international styles. Buy from a gallery, or bargain with the hawkers on the street corners or at the many open-air markets (➤ 108–109).

Goats and canoeists enjoying the Orange River

An oak wine cask in the cellars of the Western Cape

Soaking up the sun on Durban's Golden Mile

The Shaping of South Africa

3 million–100,000 years ago
Early hominids of the species *Australopithecus africanus* (Southern African ape-man) and *Homo erectus* (upright man) roam the country.

40,000 BC
South Africa's earliest fully human occupants, the Bushmen, follow a hunter-gatherer way of life. Their earliest rock art dates to 26000 BC.

300 BC
Some Bushmen acquire domesticated animals and become pastoralists, known later as the Khoikhoi ('Hottentots').

AD 250 onwards
Iron-Age Bantu-speaking people settle in northern, central and eastern South Africa.

1488–1650
Starting with Portuguese navigator Bartholomeu Dias's rounding of the Cape of Good Hope in 1488, encounters occur between the indigenous people of South Africa and Portuguese, Dutch and English explorers.

1580
Englishman Sir Francis Drake rounds the Cape.

1652
The Dutch establish a refreshment station for the Dutch East India Company trading ships passing the Cape.

1688
The number of European settlers at the Cape increases with the arrival of French Huguenots, escaping religious persecution.

1778
After repeated clashes between Dutch settlers and the Xhosa people, the Great Fish River is fixed as the eastern border of the Cape.

1795
The British occupy the Cape.

1815
Shaka, illegitimate son of a minor chief, begins to consolidate scattered tribes into the powerful Zulu kingdom.

A diamond mine, showing the cables and ladders used to descend the face

1820
Five thousand British immigrants settle in the eastern Cape.

1835–54
Dissatisfied with British rule the Afrikaner Voortrekkers leave the Cape and establish republics in the area of the present Free State, KwaZulu-Natal, Gauteng and Northern Province. They clash with the black tribes of the interior.

1860
The first indentured labourers are brought from India to work the sugar-cane plantations in Natal. Eventually 152,000 arrive, of whom half choose to remain.

1866
Diamonds are discovered near the Vaal River.

1886
Gold is discovered on the site of the future Johannesburg.

1879–87
After several wars the Zulu are defeated and their kingdom is annexed by Britain.

1893
A young Indian lawyer, Mohandas Karamchand Gandhi arrives in South Africa. After many years of political activism, he finally returns to India in 1914 where he is given the honorific 'Mahatma' (Great Soul).

1899–1902
The Anglo-Boer War is fought between Britain and the Boer republics.

1910
The various colonies and former republics of the country come together to form the Union of South Africa. But by excluding blacks the Union fails to unite all South Africans and prepares the way for many decades of black resistance.

1912
The South African Native National Congress is founded, later becoming the African National Congress (ANC).

1948
The Afrikaner-dominated National Party wins the white parliamentary election and begins to implement its policy of apartheid (racial separation).

Zulu warriors at the Battle of Rorke's Drift in 1879

1960
Police open fire on black protestors at Sharpeville, killing 69 people. ANC outlawed by the government.

1962–63
Nelson Mandela, who leads the ANC in a policy of armed resistance, is arrested and sentenced to life imprisonment on Robben Island.

1976–90
Resistance to white rule intensifies after Soweto uprising of 1976. Low-level guerrilla warfare and civil disturbances persist, and the National Party government is economically and politically isolated by the international community.

1990
President F W de Klerk lifts the ban on the ANC and other outlawed organisations. Nelson Mandela is released after 27 years in jail.

1994
South Africa's first democratic election is won by the ANC with a large majority. Nelson Mandela becomes president.

1999
The ANC increases its majority in the second election. Nelson Mandela retires, and Thabo Mbeki becomes president.

Peace & Quiet

Enjoying the view from the Western Cape's Swartberg Pass

Vast stretches of South Africa are only thinly populated, making it very easy to get away from the crowds. Within an hour or two of the major cities you can find reasonably priced hotels and bed-and-breakfast establishments. And the National Parks located in every province of South Africa provide peaceful havens for jaded city-dwellers.

Western and Eastern Cape

Just over the mountains that run parallel to the coast lies the Karoo, an expanse of semi-desert occupied only by sheep, goats and hardy farmers. Take a short break in one of the many small towns along the roads that run through the Karoo; at night in the clear dry air you will see millions of stars. Matjiesfontein offers a preserved Victorian village and hotel. Wallow in the hot springs at Montagu (➤ 43), or enjoy the absolute quiet of Nieu Bethesda (➤ 46) or Colesberg (➤ 85). Nature-lovers can soak up the stillness in the Karoo National Park near Beaufort West. Discover the small holiday resorts on the many river-mouths in the Eastern Cape, such as Port Alfred and Kenton on Sea. Harder to reach, because of the poor roads, are the deserted beaches of the Transkei Wild Coast (➤ 47).

Bright and cheerful cosmos flowers

KwaZulu-Natal, Mpumalanga & Northern Province

The eastern and northern parts of South Africa contain some of the country's finest wilderness areas. If you like mountains, the green, spectacular Drakensberg Mountains (➤ 18) are a must. If it's coastal wilderness you're after, try the Greater St Lucia Wetland (➤ 55), or the Sodwana Bay Park, with the world's most southerly tropical reefs. The only thing

likely to disturb your rest in the Kruger National Park
(➤ 22–23) is the roaring of lions and the howling of
hyenas.

If you don't feel too energetic, but would prefer to drive
from hotel to hotel through beautiful scenery, explore the
rolling hills and country towns of the KwaZulu-Natal
Midlands (➤ 56), or the areas around Hazyview and
Graskop in Mpumalanga.

Gauteng

It's not that easy to get away from the smog and the urban
sprawl in this densely populated region. One quiet spot is
the long, low range of the Magaliesberg (➤ 72), with the
Hartebeespoort Dam in the foothills, a good place for
walking, fishing, bird-watching, swimming and boat-rides.

*An angler tries his luck
from the rocks near East
London*

Northern Cape, Free State & Northwest Province

The eastern Free State, along the border of Lesotho, is
one of the most restful and beautiful parts of South Africa,
with its green hills and golden sandstone formations. The
town of Clarens, near the Golden Gate Highlands National
Park (➤ 20) is a gem. Game-watching in utter tranquillity
is possible in the huge semi-desert tracts of the Northwest
and Northern Cape. You can view wild animals from a hot-
air balloon in the Pilanesberg National Park (➤ 87), or see
antelope at the Kgalagadi Transfrontier Park (➤ 85).

*Sandstone formation in
the Golden Gate
Highlands National Park*

South Africa's Famous

Herman Charles Bosman

The writer Herman Charles Bosman (1905–51) led a dramatic life. His book *Cold Stone Jug* describes the four years he spent in gaol for the murder of his stepbrother. On his release Bosman earned his living as a journalist, editor and writer. He is best known for the famous series of stories about the 'Groot Marico' area in western South Africa which are collected in *A Cask of Jerepigo* and other volumes.

Right: *South Africa's most famous citizen, Nelson Mandela*

Below: *Nobel Laureate, Archbishop Desmond Tutu*

Olive Schreiner

One of South Africa's best known writers, Olive Schreiner (1855–1920) was born on a mission station. Her most famous book, the semi-autobiographical novel *Story of an African Farm*, was published (under an assumed male name) in 1883. Its setting was the Karoo in which she had grown up. The early-feminist heroine of the novel brought Schreiner to the attention of progressive circles in Britain. Her later novel, *Trooper Halkett of Mashonaland* (1897), criticised contemporary colonial methods in Rhodesia. Schreiner lived the last part of her life in the Karoo.

Nelson Mandela

Nelson Rolihlahla Mandela, born in the Transkei region in 1918, is South Africa's greatest statesman. He first rose to prominence in the 1950s as a founder of the ANC Youth

League, which successfully put pressure on the ANC to be more active in its opposition to white rule. When peaceful methods failed, Mandela became an advocate of armed resistance. He was convicted of conspiracy at the Rivonia Trial in 1964 and sentenced to life imprisonment. After spells on Robben Island (► 25) and in other prisons in the Western Cape, Mandela was finally released in 1990. He became the first President of a democratic South Africa following the elections of 1994, and earned the admiration and respect of many of his political adversaries. Mandela retired from public life in 1999.

Archbishop Desmond Tutu

Born in 1931, Desmond Mphilo Tutu became an Anglican clergyman in 1961. After a rapid rise through the hierarchy of the church, he became Archbishop of Cape Town between 1986 and 1996. During the years before and after this appointment, Tutu exercised crucial moral leadership, fearlessly condemning the crimes both of the apartheid regime and its opponents. For this he was awarded the Nobel Peace Prize in 1986. After retiring as archbishop, Tutu chaired South Africa's Truth and Reconciliation Commission, appointed to bring to light the abuses of the past.

Top Ten

Above: *beach huts at Muizenberg, Cape Town*
Right: *Bushman hunter in action*

1
Blyde River Canyon

 54C4

Bourke's Luck Potholes

 About 60km north of
Graskop, Mpumalanga

☎ 013-761 6019

🕐 Daily 7–5

🍴 Kiosk (£)

✈ Fly to Johannesburg

♿ Good; Lichen Trail for
the blind

👆 Cheap

❓ Mpumalanga Parks
Board ☎ 017-843 2603

Echo Caves

☎ 013-238 0015

🕐 Daily 8–5

🍴 Restaurant (££)

♿ None

👆 Moderate

*The spectacular Three
Rondavels above the
Blyde River Canyon*

*The Blyde River Canyon is a place of superb
views, soaring peaks, caves, waterfalls and a
challenging hiking trail.*

Some of South Africa's finest scenery can be found along
the Escarpment in Mpumalanga, where the interior plateau
(the Highveld) drops away dramatically to the subtropical
plains below (the Lowveld). Over the past 60 million years
the Blyde River has carved its way through the
Escarpment to form a canyon 300–800m deep.

The Blyde River Canyon proper is a 22,670ha nature
reserve, offering bird-watching, numerous walks and riding
trails, restaurants and camping in designated areas. A
40km-long, two-day hiking route runs the length of the
canyon, next to the river, but it is the spectacular views
and sights near the canyon and along its rim that are the
main attractions of the area. The Mac Mac Falls plunge
85m into a bushy gorge near to the Mac Mac Pools, a
descending series of natural basins. Also worth a visit are
the 46m Berlin Falls, on a stream that runs into the Blyde
River. At **Bourke's Luck Potholes**, at the confluence of the
Treur and Blyde rivers, you can view rocks scoured over
the millennia into weird shapes by waterborne debris.

The God's Window and Wonder View lookout points
provide magnificent panoramas of the edge of the
Escarpment and of the Lowveld eastwards as far as the
Kruger National Park (► 22–23). Don't miss the view of
the Three Rondavels, a group of hills towering over the
canyon, named for their resemblance to thatched huts.

If you're not claustrophobic, visit the **Echo Caves**,
where the stalactites resound eerily when struck.

2
Cape Peninsula

The Cape Peninsula offers extraordinary variety – beaches, mountains, wild animals – in the middle of a major city.

Breakers rolling in west of Cape Point and, inset, the tip of Cape Point

Cape Town must be one of the few major cities in the world where commuters on their way to town can view zebra and wildebeest or slip away to the beach over the lunch hour. The city's urban spread surrounds the wilderness areas of the Table Mountain chain. At many points the mountain drops away to a coastline indented to form beautiful sandy coves and bays.

The best beaches for swimming are on False Bay (at Muizenberg, Fish Hoek, The Boulders), where the water is several degrees warmer than on the western side of the Peninsula. The beaches at Clifton and Camps Bay, where the water is colder, are scenic and ideal for sunbathing.

The Cape is home to an amazing variety of plant life internationally classified as the sixth Floral Kingdom known as Fynbos. Although the smallest in area, this floral kingdom contains the richest diversity with over 8,000 varieties, of which 5,800 are found only here. Table Mountain alone has 1,470 species – more than the whole of the British Isles.

Walkers will enjoy the network of paths that criss-cross the Peninsula's mountain chain. But be warned: several tourists have to be rescued from the mountain each year. Be sensible and make sure you take a map, water and warm clothing – even in summer.

✚ 28A1

✉ Cape Town

✖ Fly to Cape Town

ℹ Corner of Castle and Burg streets, Cape Town

☎ 021-426 4260

❓ For information on hiking and flora, contact Nature Conservation ✉ 1 Dorp Street, Cape Town ☎ 021-426 0723

3
Drakensberg

The green Drakensberg Mountains provide a haven for hikers, pony trekkers, trout fishermen and nature lovers.

 81F2

 Western KwaZulu-Natal, along the border with Lesotho

033-845 1002 (information); to book, www.kznwildlife.com

The various nature reserves are usually open during daylight hours; check www.rhino.org.za or phone for information

Most camps have facilities; phone in advance

Moderate

Lesotho (➤ 90)

High peaks and cool cascades in Central Drakensberg

Named 'Dragon Mountain' by the European settlers, the Drakensberg chain stretches along the western border of KwaZulu-Natal and into Mpumalanga. The most visited part of the chain is the Central Drakensberg, which also has the highest peaks – Injasuti (3,410m), Cathkin Peak (3,148m), Champagne Castle (3,376m) and Giant's Castle (3,314m). Other popular destinations are the 8km-broad sweep of the Amphitheatre and Mont-aux-Sources in the Northern Drakensberg, and the Sani pass into Lesotho in the south.

The 'Berg, as it is locally known, with its green slopes and cold mountain streams, provides a haven for KwaZulu-Natalians escaping the heat and humidity of the subtropical east coast. The KwaZulu-Natal Nature Conservation Service runs several nature reserves in the mountains, offering camping or accommodation in serviced chalets. You can watch bearded vultures feeding at Giant's Castle, or go trout fishing at Kamberg.

In earlier centuries, Bushmen took refuge in the Drakensberg when they were driven from the lower-lying areas by European settlers and African tribesmen. Hundreds of beautiful rock paintings of animals and humans by the Bushmen can still be seen on the walls of the caves and rock shelters in the Drakensberg.

Some of South Africa's best walking and hiking can be found in these mountains, including gentle strolls through the foothills.

4
The Garden Route

One of South Africa's greatest tourist attractions, the Garden Route runs along the coast of the south-eastern Cape through forests, lakes and farmland.

The Western Cape's Garden Route extends along the coast from Mossel Bay in the west to the Tsitsikamma Forest in the east, with the Outeniqua Mountains forming the northern border of this popular holiday area.

One of the Knysna Heads guarding the entrance to the lagoon

Driving east on the N2 from Mossel Bay you pass a superb beach at Glentana before cutting inland through rolling green fields to the country town of George. From here the N2 leads on to the resort of Wilderness, set in the middle of an extensive lakeland and wetland system. Accommodation of all types is available here – caravans, houseboats, campsites, chalets, bed-and-breakfasts and holiday farms. Next is the lovely town of **Knysna**, lying along the shores of a large lagoon. Shop here for items made from indigenous hardwoods, and enjoy the locally produced beer and oysters.

At the heart of the Garden Route is **Plettenberg Bay** ('Plett' for short), originally, and aptly, called Baia Formosa (Beautiful Bay) by the Portuguese. You can swim from golden beaches or take a boat trip to view dolphins, seals and whales.

East of Plettenberg Bay, after crossing the soaring Bloukrans River Bridge, you come to the Tsitsikamma Forest, well worth making a detour to. Along this stretch are the famous 800-year-old, 37m-tall Big Tree (a giant yellowwood) and the coastal resorts of Nature's Valley and Storm's River Mouth.

Adventure activities are available all along the Garden Route, including sea-kayaking, canoeing, hiking, mountain biking and paragliding. If you are feeling particularly adventurous, try the world's highest bungee jump (175m at full stretch) from the Bloukrans River Bridge (expensive).

The Garden Route is extremely popular with locals as well as tourists, so advance booking is essential during the high season, December to January.

✚ 28C1

✉ Southeast coast of Western Cape

✈ Fly to George

ℹ West Cape Tourism Board ✉ Corner of Castle and Burg streets
☎ 021-426 5639;
e-mail:
info@capetourism.org.za
🕐 Daily 8–6

Knysna

ℹ 14 Main Street
☎ 044-382 5510;
www.knysna-info.co.za
🕐 Daily 8–6

Plettenberg Bay

ℹ Shop 35, Melville Cnr
☎ 044-533 4065;
e-mail:
info@plettenbergbay.co.za 🕐 Daily 8–5

5
Golden Gate Highlands National Park

Formations of mellow golden sandstone create a delightful landscape in and around Golden Gate, on the border between the Free State and Lesotho.

✚ 81F3

✉ 18km east of Clarens, Free State

☎ 058-255 0012 (fax 0928)

🕐 24 hours daily

🍴 Restaurant and pub (££)

✈ Fly to Bloemfontein

ℹ Free State Tourist Office ☎ 051-430 8200

♿ None

✋ Day visitors, cheap

🔄 Eastern Highlands of Free State (➤ 89)

❓ Horse riding ☎ 058-255 0951; fishing and hiking ☎ 058-256 1559

Golden tones of grass and sandstone light up the eastern Free State

Mention to many South Africans that you are planning a trip to the Free State and you'll be told that there's nothing there except boring, open plains and *mielie* (maize) fields. Yet, while it is true that the western Free State is flat and relatively featureless, the eastern part is an enchanting area of sandstone cliffs, streams and green hills, with the Maluti Mountains of Lesotho looming in the distance.

The central attraction of this region is the Golden Gate Highlands National Park, so-called for the twin buttresses of golden sandstone that rear up either side of the park entrance. In the reserve you can see eland, oribi, red hartebeest and other antelope, as well as black eagle and bearded vulture. But it is really the landscape, rather than the wildlife, that visitors come to see.

The deep layer of soft sandstone laid down over this region has been weathered by wind and water into fantastic shapes. In many places the red, ochre and gold layers, while protected from above by a cap of harder stone, have been eroded from below to create shadowy overhangs and great mushroom formations.

Near by is the picturesque town of Clarens (➤ 89), which is increasingly popular with tourists.

6
Kimberley's Big Hole

In their frenzy to discover diamonds, miners created the world's largest man-made excavation, the Big Hole, between 1871 and 1914.

In 1869 diamonds were discovered at Bultfontein, near the place which grew into the city of Kimberley (➤ 83), in the Northern Cape. Two years later the diamond-diggers' attention shifted to an insignificant-looking nearby hillock, Colesberg Koppie. Very soon the hill had disappeared into a huge pit.

What the diggers had stumbled on was the mouth of an enormous, ancient volcanic vent filled with a bluish clay-like substance, a so-called kimberlite pipe. This one was extraordinarily rich in diamonds. Over the 43 years that the pipe was worked no fewer than 2,720kg of diamonds were taken from it. All that was left here when the mining stopped was the 800m-deep Big Hole.

Even today, when it is filled with water to within 174m of the top, the Big Hole is an awe-inspiring sight, with a circumference of 1.6km, and a surface area of more than 13ha. But take a look at the old black-and-white photographs of the diggings, on view in the Kimberley Mine Museum (➤ 84) on the rim of the hole. Here you get a real sense of what it was like in the old days, with hundreds of aerial ropeways reaching down from the edge of the pipe to the masses of diggers below.

✚ 81D3

✉ Tucker Street, Kimberley, Northern Cape

☎ 053-839 4901/2

🕐 Daily, summer 8–6; winter 8–4

🍴 Restaurant (£)

✈ Fly to Kimberley

ℹ Kimberley Tourist Office ✉ 121 Bultfontein Street ☎ 053-832 7298; e-mail: tourism@kbymun.org.za

♿ Phone in advance

✋ Moderate

Kimberley's Big Hole, now three-quarters filled with water

7
Kruger National Park

 54C4

 Mpumalanga and Northern Province

 012-428 9111; e-mail: reservations@parks-sa.co.za

 Daily, daylight hours

Restaurant, café, shop in all main camps (£)

Fly to Johannesburg; flights into Skukuza available ☎ 011-978 5413

Phone in advance

Day admission moderate; accommodation from cheap to very expensive

Blyde River Canyon (➤ 16); Pilgrim's Rest (➤ 61, 62); Barberton (➤ 60); Letaba District (➤ 60); Sudwala Caves (➤ 62); Venda (➤ 62)

Book for walking trails one year in advance; night drives and day trails available from most camps

The Kruger National Park is one of the oldest and most famous nature reserves in the world, with an astonishing variety of flora and fauna.

The Kruger National Park overwhelms with its sheer size. Stretching 350km from the Limpopo River in the north to the Sabie River in the south, and on average 60km wide, the park covers nearly 2,000,000ha, a territory the size of Wales.

The names of two men especially are inextricably linked with the creation of the park. The President of the old Transvaal Republic, Paul Kruger, had an area on the Sabie River declared a government reserve in 1898. (This was the world's second such wilderness area, after Yellowstone in the USA, proclaimed in 1872.)

During his 44 years in charge, Major James Stevenson-Hamilton, a dedicated conservationist, warded off poachers, mining companies and farmers in search of grazing from the park. He tirelessly extended the territory of the reserve until it almost reached its present size, and it was under his guidance that the area was declared the Kruger National Park in 1926.

Today the park is made up of three distinct habitats: the southern region around the ever-popular Skukuza, with deciduous trees and tall grasses; the central region, mainly open savannah, accessible through the Phalaborwa and Orpen gates; and miles of *mopane* scrub in the north around Shingwedzi and Punda Maria. Many animals can be seen in all three regions, but rhino favour the south and grazing animals the central savannah, while the shattered, but hardy, *mopane* trees of the north are evidence of the many elephant there.

The Kruger National Park is very definitely a place that belongs to animals rather than humans. Visitors must stay on the tarred main roads and gravel secondary roads, but these give access to only a fraction of the park's total area. Although the Kruger is home to nearly 150 types of mammal, over 100 species of reptile and more than 500 species of bird, there is no guarantee what you will find on any particular visit.

Everyone wants to see the Big Five: lion, buffalo, elephant, rhino and leopard. But visiting the park is also about getting in touch with your surroundings and being observant of small things, such as plants, birds and insects. Keep your

A magnificent black-maned lion keeps watch from the shade

eyes wide open, but remember that hearing and smell are just as important as good eyesight for tracking animals.

For a different view of the Kruger try one of the night drives now offered by all the main camps. If you have the time (and book well in advance) you can even go on a walking safari, accompanied by an armed ranger.

A wide variety of accommodation is available in the park's 20 or so camps. You can stay in expensive, air-conditioned luxury chalets, or in more moderately priced rondavels (thatched round huts). Alternatively you can rough it cheaply in a tent. But whatever option you choose you should book as far in advance as possible.

There are several essential dos and don'ts. Never disturb the animals – remember it's their home not yours. Never get out of your vehicle, except at designated viewpoints; even here you do so at your own risk. When stopping to look at potentially dangerous animals, always stop beyond them and look back – it's easier to get away in forward gear than in reverse.

Olifants Lodge in the western region of the Kruger National Park

Elephants and Burchell's zebras, showing off their pyjama stripes, are a highlight of any visit to Kruger National Park

8
Namaqualand Flowers

Dazzling wild flowers carpet the veld near Kamieskroon

In springtime the arid west coast of South Africa explodes with colour as the year's new wild flowers appear.

✚ 80A2

✉ From Saldanha Bay, Western Cape, north to Springbok, Northern Cape

☎ Flower Line (cell) 083-910 1028

✈ Fly to Cape Town

ℹ Springbok Tourist Office ☎ 027-718 2986

Postberg Nature Reserve

☎ 02277-22144

 Moderate

South Africa's west coast from just north of Cape Town all the way up to Springbok in Namaqualand is harsh, bone-dry territory. Yet from mid-August to mid-September most years an astonishing phenomenon occurs. If the winter rains have been sufficiently heavy, and the spring is not too hot, the landscape comes alive with millions of yellow, white and purple flowers.

You don't have to go far off the beaten track to see the flowers. The **Postberg Nature Reserve** (open only during the flower season), just one hour's drive north of Cape Town, offers excellent viewing opportunities. An added attraction here are the wild animals: zebra, ostrich, jackal and around ten species of antelope.

But the most spectacular displays of flowers are to be found further north, in Namaqualand, in the region around Kamieskroon and Springbok. Though a saloon car is perfectly adequate for a flower tour, a number of 4x4 trails have opened recently in Namaqualand, giving access to the remoter parts of this already remote area.

Flowers include the scarlet, yellow, purple and white blossoms of the ubiquitous succulents (mesembryan-themums), several varieties of lily, aloes and field after field of Namaqualand daisies.

9
Robben Island

Half-an-hour by boat from Cape Town harbour lies historic Robben Island, where Nelson Mandela was imprisoned.

Robben Island consists of a bleak 574ha of low-lying, wind-swept scrub. What draws hundreds of thousands of tourists here each year is not its scenic beauty but the rich history of the island and the magnificent views it affords of the Cape Peninsula.

Robben (Dutch for 'seals') Island has served as a place of confinement for society's outcasts ever since the coming of European settlers. Already in the 17th century Jan van Riebeeck banished a local rebel, Autshumato, to the island. Prominent Xhosa and Islamic leaders followed in later centuries. In the 1800s Robben Island became an asylum for mental patients and then a leper colony.

But it was as a gaol for apartheid's political prisoners after 1963 that Robben Island achieved its greatest notoriety. Many of those in the present African National Congress government were inmates on 'the Island', as was the leader of the Pan-Africanist Congress, Robert Sobukwe. Most famous of all its prisoners was Nelson Mandela (➤ 14), detained here from 1964 until 1982.

Robben Island is a restricted area, which you can visit only as part of an official tour. Starting by boat from Cape Town's Waterfront (➤ 26), you land at Murray's Harbour. Highlights are the visit to the prison and Mandela's cell; the viewpoint from which you can see a fine panorama of the Cape Peninsula; and the island's colony of jackass penguins.

➕ 28A1

✉ 9km off coast of Cape Town, Western Cape

☎ 021-413-4200 (Tour Line); fax: 021-419 1057

🚤 Boats leave on the hour, 8–3 daily from the Clock Tower, Victoria and Alfred Waterfront

♿ Wheelchairs accommodated

✋ Expensive

↔ Victoria and Alfred Waterfront (➤ 26)

Below: *an arial view of Murray's Harbour and Robben Island*
Inset: *the Victorian Guest House on Robben Island dates back to 1895*

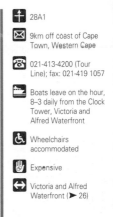

10
Victoria and Alfred Waterfront, Cape Town

A complex of specialist shops, cinemas, museums, restaurants and hotels makes up Cape Town's ever-popular Victoria and Alfred Waterfront.

✚ 33C5

✉ Dock Road, Cape Town, Western Cape

☎ 021-408 7600 (information); fax: 021-408 7605; e-mail: info@waterfront.co.za

 Restaurants, pubs open daily till late; shops open daily, 9–9

🍴 Huge variety to choose from (£–£££)

🚌 Buses from Cape Town Station and Sea Point

♿ Very good

 Free

↔ Robben Island (➤ 25)

❓ Phone for details of musical and other events

Victoria and Alfred Waterfront against the magnificent backdrop of Table Mountain

In just ten years, from the early 1990s, a handful of rundown buildings in Cape Town harbour have metamorphosed into the country's premier tourist attraction, the Victoria and Alfred Waterfront. Several factors contribute to its success: the architecture and the superb views, but perhaps most important of all, the peculiar charm of the combination of genuine working harbour and leisure spot.

The Waterfront offers a wide spectrum of entertainment – a choice of cinemas, one with a five-storey-high IMAX screen, a theatre, a sports café, nightclubs, and music venues, the best-known being the Green Dolphin for jazz. In summer you can watch buskers and listen to live music in the outdoor amphitheatre. The complex also has dozens of eating places, ranging from fast-food outlets, to steakhouses, pizzerias, seafood bars and expensive restaurants. The most atmospheric of the pubs is Ferryman's Tavern, housed in a converted warehouse.

Although prices in the shops here seem expensive to locals, they are reasonable if you are spending US dollars or European currencies. Outlets offer books, clothing of all sorts, fine foods and wines, electrical goods, gifts, local art and curios. There are also several indoor craft markets.

Other places of interest at the Waterfront include the South African Maritime Museum, the floating Victoria Museum Ship, the Two Oceans Aquarium (➤ 39), and the platform next to Bertie's Landing where Cape fur seals bask. Various tours are available from here, too: a sunset cruise in Table Bay, helicopter flights over the Peninsula, and trips around and to Robben Island (➤ 25).

What
To See

Above: humans and jackass penguins mingle at The Boulders, near Simon's Town
Right: a Ndebele woman in traditional finery

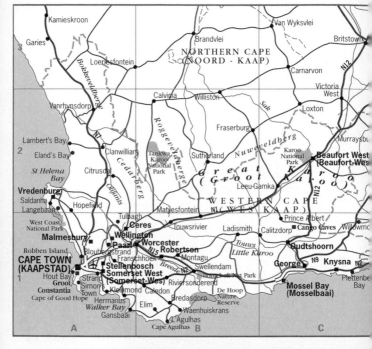

Colourful fishing boats, sandy beach, rolling breakers – a typical scene on the Western Cape coast

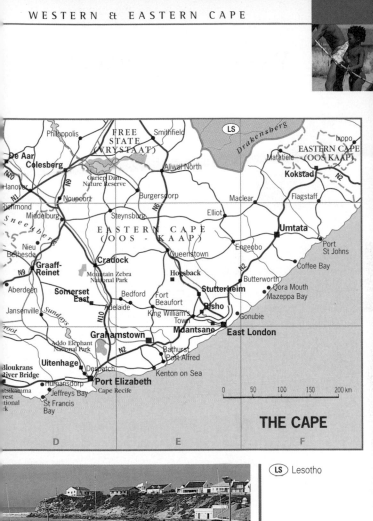

THE CAPE

LS Lesotho

Western & Eastern Cape

Unlike the rest of South Africa, the Western Cape has a Mediterranean climate, with mild, wet winters and hot, dry summers. As this region was the earliest to be occupied by European settlers, some of the oldest towns and buildings in the country are here. Visitors come to enjoy the sheer natural beauty of the Cape, hike in its mountains, tour its wine farms, soak up the atmosphere of its small country towns and relax on its beaches.

The superbly scenic Garden Route provides a gateway from the Western into the Eastern Cape, a region steeped in a history of contact and conflict between the Xhosa people and European settlers. Grahamstown will fascinate those interested in the past, while nature-lovers will want to head for the Addo Elephant National Park and the vast empty beaches of the Wild Coast.

> ‘ *This Cape is the most stately thing and the fairest Cape we saw in the whole circumference of the earth.* ’
>
> SIR FRANCIS DRAKE
> (on the Cape Peninsula),
> *Journal* (1580)

Cape Town

Cape Town's colourful history and combination of mountains and sea make it one of the most attractive cities in the world. Known affectionately as the Mother City, it is by far the oldest urban centre in South Africa. In 1652 the Dutch East India Company sent Jan van Riebeeck here to establish a fresh-produce garden (the Company's Garden, ➤ 34) to supply its passing ships. The small way station grew gradually into a town, then into a city, passing from Dutch to British control in 1795. After the formation of the Union in 1910, Cape Town became, and remains, the legislative capital of the country and seat of Parliament.

First contact: Jan van Riebeeck lands at the Cape

Present-day Cape Town is a cosmopolitan place, populated by a mix of peoples descended from the indigenous Khoi, slaves originally brought here from Indonesia, Angola, Madagascar and Mozambique, settlers from many countries of Europe and, increasingly, Xhosa-speaking people from the Eastern Cape.

Superbly situated at the foot of Table Mountain, the city offers many things to do and see: mountain walks, swimming from beautiful beaches, scenic drives, museums, art galleries, historic monuments and many restaurants and music venues. Once you have exhausted the

pleasures of Cape Town, there is plenty to enjoy in the surrounding region. Within a day's drive of the city you can sample wines and have lunch under the oaks at the farms along the Wine Route, watch whales at Hermanus (➤ 43), see the spring flowers to the north (➤ 24), and visit beautiful towns such as Stellenbosch and Tulbagh (➤ 44).

The range of the Twelve Apostles overlooking the white sands of Camps Bay

What to See in Cape Town

33A1

✉ Corner of Government
Avenue and Orange Street

☎ 021-424 9381

🕐 Tue–Thu 10–4:30. Closed
Good Friday, 25 Dec

🍴 Café (££)

✋ Cheap

♿ Few

33A2

Bo-Kaap Museum

✉ 71 Wale Street

☎ 021-481 3939

🕐 Mon–Sat 9:30–4:30

✋ Cheap

♿ None

33C2

✉ Buitenkant Street

☎ 021-464 1272; fax: 021-
464 1280; e-mail:
castle@cis.co.za

🕐 9–4; Dec–Jan
Mon–Sat 9–5

🍴 Café (£)

♿ Good

✋ Cheap

↔ District Six
Museum
(➤ 34)

❓ Phone for
details of
guided tours,
open days

Above: a *minaret above
the Bo-Kaap*
Right: *Castle of Good
Hope as seen from the
courtyard*

BERTRAM HOUSE ✪

This Georgian redbrick house, a unique survival in Cape Town, was built by an English attorney-builder, John Barker, in the 1830s. It is now an off-shoot of the Slave Lodge (➤ 38) and houses a collection of fine furniture, *objets d'art*, silver and ceramics. The house and its contents give a good impression of what everyday life was like for a well-to-do English family at the Cape in the 19th century.

BO-KAAP ✪✪

The Bo-Kaap (Upper-Cape) or Malay Quarter lies on the steep slopes of Signal Hill, directly above the city. In the 19th century it became, and remains today, a predominantly Muslim area. At the **Bo-Kaap Museum** you will get a vivid impression of the life of the Muslim community, its contribution to the making of the Afrikaans language and to Cape culture. Walking tours of the picturesque cobbled streets and brightly coloured terraced cottages of the Bo-Kaap start from the museum.

CASTLE OF GOOD HOPE ✪✪

The pentagonal layout and five angled bastions of the Castle of Good Hope were the latest in military architecture when it was begun in 1666. Completed in 1679, the Castle is the oldest European building in South Africa.

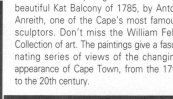

The central courtyard gives access to the beautiful Kat Balcony of 1785, by Anton Anreith, one of the Cape's most famous sculptors. Don't miss the William Fehr Collection of art. The paintings give a fascinating series of views of the changing appearance of Cape Town, from the 17th to the 20th century.

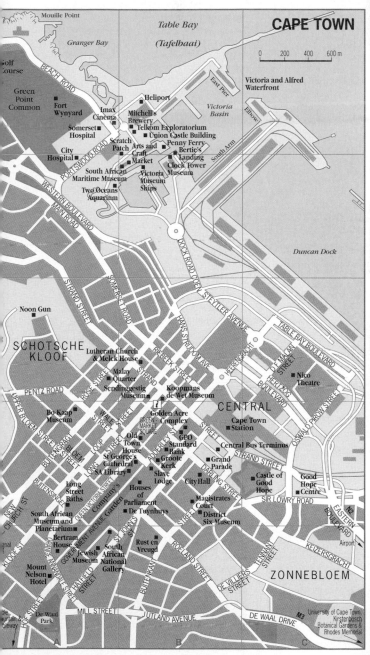

CAPE TOWN

Mouille Point

Table Bay
(Tafelbaai)

Granger Bay

Victoria and Alfred
Waterfront

0   200   400   600 m

Golf
Course

Green
Point
Common

BEACH ROAD

East Pier

Victoria
Basin

Elbow

South Arm

Heliport

Fort
Wynyard

Imax
Cinema

Mitchell's
Brewery

Telkom Exploratorium

Union Castle Building

Penny Ferry

Somerset
Hospital

Scratch
Patch

Arts and
Craft
Market

Bertie's
Landing

City
Hospital

South African
Maritime Museum

Victoria
Museum
Ships

Clock Tower
Museum

Two Oceans
Aquarium

Duncan Dock

PORTSWOOD ROAD

WESTERN BOULEVARD

MAIN ROAD

DOCK ROAD

OSWALD

STEYTLER AVENUE

HANS STRIJDOM AVE

Noon Gun

STRAND STREET

SOMERSET ROAD

HERTZOG BOULEVARD

TABLE BAY BOULEVARD

DE MAGA

SCHOTSCHE
KLOOF

Lutheran Church
& Melck House

BREE STREET

Nico
Theatre

UPPER BLOEM STREET

PENTZ ROAD

ROSE STREET

Malay
Quarter

STRAND

Sendinggestig
Museum

Koopmans
de Wet Museum

CENTRAL

Bo-Kaap
Museum

WALE STREET

Golden Acre
Complex

Cape Town
Station

BUITENGRACHT STREET

BLOEM STREET

LOOP STREET

GREEN
MARKET
SQUARE

Old
Town
House

ADDERLEY STREET

GPO

Standard
Bank

STRAND STREET

Central Bus Terminus

St George's
Cathedral

Groote
Kerk

Grand
Parade

DARLING STREET

Castle of
Good
Hope

Good
Hope
Centre

SA Library

Slave
Lodge

City Hall

Long
Street
Baths

BUITENSINGEL

QUEEN VICTORIA STREET

Houses of
Parliament

De Tuynhuys

Company's
Garden

Magistrates
Court

District
Six Museum

SIR LOWRY ROAD

EASTERN BOULEVARD

N2

NEW CHURCH ST

KLOOF ST

South African
Museum and
Planetarium

Bertram
House

GOVERNMENT AVENUE

ST JOHN'S STREET

Rust en
Vreugd

ROELAND STREET

Airport

KEIZERSGRACHT

Jewish
Museum

South
African
National
Gallery

DE VILLERS STREET

TENNANT STREET

M3

Mount
Nelson
Hotel

HATFIELD STREET

BOUWMANT

ZONNEBLOEM

De Waal
Park

MILL STREET

JUTLAND AVENUE

DE WAAL DRIVE

University of Cape Town,
Kirstenbosch
Botanical Gardens &
Rhodes Memorial

A   B   C

33

33A2

Government Avenue

7–sunset

Tea room (£)

Free

Slave Lodge, South African Library (➤ 38), South African Museum (➤ 38), South African National Gallery (➤ 39)

33B2

Methodist Church, Buitenkant Street

021-461 8745 (also fax)

Mon–Sat 9–4. Closed 1 Jan, Good Fri, 25 Dec

Very good

Cheap

Castle of Good Hope (➤ 32)

33B2

Flea market

Corner of Burg and Longmarket streets

Mon–Sat 9–4

Good

Michaelis Collection

Corner of Longmarket and Burg streets

021-481 3933

Mon–Fri 10–5, Sat 10–4

Cheap

Right: *bargain-hunting in Greenmarket Square*
Below: *a map of District Six on the museum floor*

COMPANY'S GARDEN ✪✪✪

The garden Jan van Riebeeck established for the Dutch East India Company in the 17th century is still in place – though lawns, roses and indigenous trees grow there now rather than the original fruit and vegetables. Tree-shaded Government Avenue runs the whole length of the Garden, giving access to its museums and galleries. Situated in the heart of the city, it is a place where you can relax, feed the squirrels and pigeons, and enjoy a drink or a light meal at the open-air restaurant.

DISTRICT SIX MUSEUM ✪

District Six, on the edge of central Cape Town, was the site of a vibrant working-class community which was destroyed by the apartheid laws in the 1960s and 70s. The inhabitants of the area were forcibly removed and their houses bulldozed to make way for a white suburb, but such was the opposition to this action that most of the land has since remained unoccupied. The District Six Museum commemorates this episode in history with a wealth of photographs and other documentation.

GREENMARKET SQUARE ✪✪

Greenmarket Square's name indicates its origins. Laid out as a fresh produce market in 1710, today it is a pleasant, tree-shaded space housing a **flea market**. Weather permitting, you can bargain here most days of the year for jewellery, knick-knacks, crafts, artworks, curios and clothing. The attractive 18th-century building on the southwest side of the square is the Old Town House. Formerly a town hall, it now houses the outstanding **Michaelis Collection** of early Dutch and Flemish painting.

GROOTE KERK

The origins of the Groote Kerk (Big Church), the mother church of the Dutch Reformed Church in South Africa, go back to 1704, when the first building on the site was inaugurated. This simple thatched structure was replaced in 1841 by the present church; only the old clock tower remains. One of the most striking features is the church's fine wooden pulpit, carved in 1789 by Anton Anreith and Jan Graaff.

🟦 33B2
✉ 39 Adderley Street
☎ 021-461 7044; fax: 021-461 7620
🕐 Mon–Fri 10–2
💵 Free
↔ Slave Lodge (► 38)
❓ Guided tours

The neo-classical portico of the Houses of Parliament

HOUSES OF PARLIAMENT

Dating back to 1884, the Houses of Parliament have been modified several times to accommodate successive political dispensations. Today they house the legislature of the fully representative government first elected in 1994. Sessions of parliament are open to the public during the first half of the year; in the second half, guided tours are available of the buildings and their gallery of historical paintings and parliamentary memorabilia.

🟦 33B2
✉ Parliament Street
☎ 021-403 2911
🕐 Open daily; tours only available weekdays
♿ Good
💵 Free
❓ Hourly guided tours; phone for details

LONG STREET

Aptly named Long Street runs the whole length of Cape Town, from sea to mountain. Alternately seedy and striking, the street is becoming increasingly the home of agents and lodges catering for budget travellers. There are also churches, a mosque, second-hand bookshops, louche all-night bars, clubs and cafés, tattoo parlours, sex shops and junk emporia. Long Street is a wonderful gallery of late Victorian commercial architecture displaying many interesting details in plaster, wrought iron, ceramic and stonework. The interior of the **Long Street Baths**, at the head of the street, is in classic Edwardian style, and you can have a swim, Turkish bath or massage here.

🟦 33A2

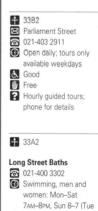

Long Street Baths
☎ 021-400 3302
🕐 Swimming, men and women: Mon–Sat 7AM–8PM, Sun 8–7 (Tue 10–4 women only)
♿ Good, lift into pool
💵 Cheap to moderate
❓ Steam baths and massage available, phone for details

35

33B3
✉ 19 Buitengraght Street
☎ 021-421 5854; fax: 021-461 9620
🕐 Mon, Wed, Fri 10–2
♿ Good
💲 Free
↔ Greenmarket Square (► 34)

33B1
✉ 78 Buitenkant Street
☎ 021-464 3280; fax: 021-461 9620; e-mail: wfehr@iafrica.co.za
🕐 Mon–Fri 8:30–4:30
♿ None
💲 Cheap

33B2
✉ 5 Wale Street
☎ 021-424 7360; fax: 021-423 8466; e-mail: vestry@mweb.co.za
🕐 Mon–Fri 6:30–6, Sat 7–noon, Sun 6:30–noon
♿ Ramp
💲 Free
↔ Company's Garden (► 34)

LUTHERAN CHURCH AND PARSONAGE ⭐

The ubiquitous Anton Anreith had a hand in both these buildings, as carver of the striking wooden pulpit in the Lutheran Church and as architect of the adjoining parsonage. The church was built by the wealthy merchant, Martin Melck, in 1774, shortly after freedom of worship was granted to the Lutherans at the Cape. The handsome building next door, now in use as offices, was originally the parsonage.

RUST EN VREUGD ⭐

The William Fehr Collection of art relating to South Africa is divided between the Castle (► 32) and Rust en Vreugd (Rest and Joy). But it is not only the display of furniture, paintings, and watercolours by Thomas Baines that is worth seeing here. The house itself, with its beautiful proportions and handsome pillared porch, is one of the best examples of 18th-century domestic architecture in Cape Town. The formal garden is modelled on Cape Dutch gardens of the period.

ST GEORGE'S CATHEDRAL ⭐

The present Anglican cathedral, designed by architect Sir Herbert Baker, was completed in 1901, replacing the original building of 1834. The grey neo-Gothic edifice, a little bit of England in Africa, is more impressive inside than outside. Particularly striking are the modern stained-glass windows depicting the Creation, and the 8m rose window by Francis Spear. The window above the transept is dedicated to Lord Louis Mountbatten. St George's most famous incumbent was Archbishop Desmond Tutu (► 14), who retired in 1996.

Above: *Rust en Vreugd amid its formal gardens*
Right: *Cape Gothic: St George's Cathedral*

Around Historic Cape Town Centre

This walk takes you right through the heart of the old city.

Start from the Grand Parade, between the Castle (➤ 32) and the City Hall.

The ornate 1905 City Hall overlooks the Grand Parade, where 100,000 people came to hear Nelson Mandela (➤ 14) speak on his release from prison.

Walk along Strand Street and turn left into Adderley Street.

Walking along Adderley, Cape Town's main street, you will see on your left flower-sellers, the grand 19th-century Standard Bank, the Groote Kerk (➤ 35) and the Slave Lodge (➤ 38).

Continue on straight up Government Avenue pedestrian way.

To your left is the back of Parliament and the stately Tuynhuys, now the State President's office. If you detour a little to your right you will find yourself in the heart of the Company's Garden (➤ 34).

Turn right across the front of the South African Museum (➤ 38), left up Grey's Pass, right into Orange, and then right again into Long Street (➤ 35).

If you are feeling tired you can relax at the Baths here. Otherwise go window-shopping or sit and enjoy something to drink at one of the many bars and cafés.

Go down Long Street, turn right into Church Street, then left into Burg, right into Longmarket, down the side of Greenmarket Square (➤ 34), and then left along the pedestrian precinct of St George's Mall.

This is the heart of commercial Cape Town. In summer the area is alive with buskers, street-traders and shoppers.

Turn right into Strand, which will take you back to the Grand Parade.

Distance
3km

Time
1 hour without stops, 3 hours with stops

Start/end point
Grand Parade
✚ 33B2

Tea or lunch
Tea room in Company's Garden (£)
✉ Off Government Avenue
☎ 021-423 2919

City Hall's handsome clock tower

DID YOU KNOW?

A cannon is fired every day on Signal Hill above Cape Town to announce the hour of noon.

✚ 33B2
✉ 49 Adderley Street
☎ 021-460 8240; fax: 021-460 8202
www.museums.org.za/iziko
🕓 Mon–Sat 9:3–4:30
♿ None
💷 Cheap
↔ Groote Kerk (► 35)

✚ 33B2
✉ 5 Queen Victoria Street
☎ 021-424 6320
🕓 Mon–Fri 2–5
♿ Good
💷 Free
↔ Company's Garden (► 34)

✚ 33A1
✉ 25 Queen Victoria Street
☎ 021-481 3800; fax: 021-481 3993
🕓 Museum 10–5
🍴 Café (££)
♿ Good
💷 Cheap; Wed free
❓ Phone for details of Planetarium shows
☎ 021-481 3900

The South African Museum (below) houses rock paintings of graceful antelope (inset)

SLAVE LODGE ◎◎

First built in 1685, this handsome white building has had a varied history as a slave lodge, brothel, Supreme Court and now a museum of cultural history. The collection includes not only extensive materials illustrating the cultures of the different communities in South Africa, but also objects from elsewhere in the world, including coins, weaponry and some fine Greek and Roman vases. Parts of the collection are displayed at Bertram House (► 32) and the Bo-Kaap Museum (► 32).

SOUTH AFRICAN LIBRARY ◎

Founded in 1818, this was one of the earliest free libraries in the world. A donation of books provided its first stock, and it was maintained till 1829 by a tax on wine. One of its greatest treasures is the collection of 5,000 volumes given by Sir George Grey, a former governor of the Cape, which includes illuminated medieval manuscripts. Exhibitions from the collection are held regularly in the library.

SOUTH AFRICAN MUSEUM AND PLANETARIUM ◎◎

This museum, the oldest on the subcontinent, was opened in 1825, and moved to its present building in 1897; it was originally housed in what is now the Slave Lodge (► above). The main emphases here are on the anthropology, implements and art of Southern Africa's earliest inhabitants, as well as natural history, animals, fossils and geology. You can listen to recorded whale sounds in the ever-popular Whale Hall, while viewing the skeletons of a variety of these huge mammals hanging from the ceiling. The adjoining Planetarium offers regularly changing shows of the Southern hemisphere's night skies and evening lectures.

SOUTH AFRICAN NATIONAL GALLERY ✪✪

In former years this gallery displayed mainly European art, and its earlier collection included paintings by 17th-century Italian masters and works by Stubbs and Victorian painters. But more recently the gallery has concentrated on South African art: international-style paintings and sculpture, photography, so-called 'township art' and traditional art-forms such as beadwork. The gallery regularly holds excellent temporary exhibitions.

✚	33A1
✉	Government Avenue, Company's Garden
☎	021-467 4660
🕐	Tue–Sun 10–5. Closed 1 May
🍴	Café (££)
♿	Good
💷	Cheap

TABLE MOUNTAIN AND CABLEWAY ✪✪✪

Table Mountain towers dramatically 1,086m above Cape Town. A good stiff walk will get you to the top and back again in about five hours. The recently upgraded cableway takes the less energetic to the top in five minutes, with the large cable-cars revolving through 360 degrees to give a panoramic outlook. Visitors can ramble over the almost flat 'tabletop' to enjoy the fabulous views which open up in every direction. In summer look out for the spectacular 'tablecloth' of cloud which often spreads over the mountain.

✚	33A1
✉	Tafelberg Road
☎	021-424 0015; www.tablemountain.net
🕐	Generally daylight hours; Dec–Jan 7:30AM–10PM; phone for seasonal variations
🍴	Restaurant and café (££)
♿	Good
💷	Expensive

TWO OCEANS AQUARIUM ✪✪✪

This beautiful aquarium concentrates on marine life from the two oceans said to meet at Cape Point, the Indian and the Atlantic. Its tanks display commercial fish such as yellowtail and snoek (a kind of mackerel), and brilliantly coloured tropical species, as well as sharks, moray eels, penguins and seals. A highlight is the kelp forest waving hypnotically to and fro in a huge, round tank, nearly 10m high. Upstairs is a display showing the ecology of rivers, and a tank where children can touch various marine species, such as anemones and starfish.

✚	33A4
✉	Dock Road, Victoria and Alfred Waterfront
☎	021-418 3823
🕐	9:30–6
🍴	Restaurant (££) ☎ 021-419 9068
♿	Good
💷	Expensive

VICTORIA AND ALFRED WATERFRONT (► 26, TOP TEN)

Above: *cloud shrouds Devil's Peak behind the SA National Gallery*

39

Around Cape Peninsula

Distance
110km

Time
3 hours (depending on traffic) without stops, 6 hours with stops

Start/end point
Cape Town city centre
✚ 28A1

Lunch or tea
Camel Rock Restaurant(£–££)
✉ Scarborough
☎ 021-780 1122

Mariner's Wharf (£–££)
✉ Hout Bay
☎ 021-790 1100

The Boulders, a favourite resort for people and penguins

The most scenic parts of the Cape Peninsula can be seen on this drive.

Take the M3 out of the city and keep following the directions to Muizenberg.

You will pass Groote Schuur Hospital (left), site of the world's first heart-transplant, and the whitewashed Mostert's Mill (left), before climbing over Wynberg Hill and down into the Constantia Valley.

After about 18km the M3 ends at a T-junction. Turn left on to the M42, then right at the next T-junction on to the Main Road (M4). Keep to this road as it skirts Muizenberg and then winds along the False Bay coast through Fish Hoek to Simon's Town.

If you have the time (and it's not windy), Muizenberg and Fish Hoek have excellent swimming beaches. Simon's Town, home of the South African Navy, is worth visiting for its delightful Victorian shopfronts and pleasant waterfront development on the harbour.

Going south from Simon's Town on the M4 you soon reach the turn-off to The Boulders (left).

At The Boulders, a pretty beach set among huge granite boulders, you should stop to view the fascinating jackass penguin colony on the beach.

Continue south on the M4 until the road climbs away from the sea, becoming the M65, and reaches the turn-off (left) to the Cape of Good Hope Nature Reserve and Cape Point.

If you have the time, make the detour through the nature

reserve to visit Cape Point; the restaurant there offers stunning panoramic views over False Bay.

Keep following the M65 across the peninsula to the other side. Skirting the Atlantic coast via Scarborough and Kommetjie you reach Sun Valley. Turn left here and follow the M64 (Ou Kaapse Weg, 'Old Cape Road') over the mountain. (At the time of writing the beautifully scenic M6 from Sun Valley via Chapman's Peak to Hout Bay was to be re-opened shortly. Take it if it is open.)

The most southerly point of Africa is not Cape Point, but Cape Agulhas, some 250km southeast of Cape Town.

At the highest point of the Ou Kaapse Weg you will see the entrance (left) to the Silvermine Nature Reserve. There are easy walking paths around the picturesque dam.

When the Ou Kaapse Weg ends at a T-junction turn left on to the M42 and continue on it until you come to the M41. Turn left here and drive along the winding road that climbs up to Constantia Nek.

Soon after turning on to the M42, pass Pollsmoor Prison (right) where Nelson Mandela spent several years. Drive through Tokai Forest and the vineyards of Constantia. On the M41 is the turn-off (left) to Groot Constantia (➤ 42).

From Constantia Nek descend via the M63 to Hout Bay.

Stop at Hout Bay for seafood at Mariner's Wharf. There are boat trips from here to nearby Duiker Island, where you can see seals, bank cormorants, Cape cormorants, Cape gannets, kelp gulls and arctic skuas.

Swimmers alongside a bright beach hut on the pure white sands of Muizenburg

The M6, a coastal road with magnificent views, takes you from Hout Bay past Llandudno to Camps Bay.

Both Llandudno and Camps Bay have beautiful, white, sandy beaches, ideal for sunbathing, but very cold water.

Just past Camps Bay turn right off the M6 on to Lower Kloof Road, then very soon sharp right on to Kloof Road. This takes you through the 'Glen' up to Kloof Nek. From there descend via Kloof Nek Road back down to the city.

Groot Constantia, a gem of Cape Dutch architecture

✚ 28A1
✉ Off the M41, Constantia
☎ 021-795 5140; fax: 021-795 5150
🕐 10–5
🍴 Tavern (££); Jonkershuis (£££)
♿ Good
💷 Cheap

✚ 33C1
✉ Rhodes Drive
☎ 021-799 8899
🕐 Summer 8–7; winter 8–6
🍴 Restaurant and café (££)
♿ Very good
💷 Moderate

Protea in full bloom at Kirstenbosch

✚ 33C1
✉ Off Rhodes Drive, on Groote Schuur Estate
🕐 Daylight hours
💷 Free
🍴 Rhodes Memorial Restaurant 🕐 9–5 ☎ 021-689 9151
♿ None
💷 Moderate

What to See Around Cape Town

GROOT CONSTANTIA ✪✪

Groot (Great) Constantia is one of the oldest wine estates in South Africa, having been granted to Governor Simon van der Stel in 1685. The Cape Dutch manor house with its collection of period furniture, silverware and ceramics dates back originally to the 17th century. It was gutted by fire in 1925, but has been faithfully restored. The wine cellar, with pedimental sculpture by Anton Anreith, was built in the late 1700s and is now a wine museum.

KIRSTENBOSCH ✪✪✪

Kirstenbosch is among the world's finest botanical gardens, and contains nearly 7,000 species, of which about 900 occur naturally in the unplanted areas of the garden. In the planted areas look out for the magnificent proteas, cycads, restios, succulents and aloes. The conservatory houses desert species and baobabs, and don't miss the magical, crystal-clear pool, Colonel Bird's Bath, in its secluded dell, with tree ferns overhanging it. The shop sells plants, souvenirs and books. Concerts are held on the lawns on Sunday afternoons in summer, and there is a braille trail and scent garden for the blind.

RHODES MEMORIAL ✪

Perched on the slopes of Devil's Peak, this classical-style memorial to the mining magnate, politician and imperialist Cecil Rhodes (1853–1902) is a favourite resort for Capetonians. The views are magnificent, children clamber over the huge bronze lions and visitors take lunch at the charming restaurant. The imposing granite monument was designed by Rhodes's favourite architect, Sir Herbert Baker. G F Watts sculpted the dramatic equestrian statue here called *Energy*, and Rudyard Kipling composed the poem inscribed below the bust of Rhodes.

ROBBEN ISLAND (► 25, TOP TEN)

What to See in the Western Cape

GARDEN ROUTE (► 19, TOP TEN)

HERMANUS ✪✪
This popular seaside resort offers good beaches, a busy flea market, restaurants and walks in the nearby Fernkloof Nature Reserve. But the major attraction is the southern right whales which come annually to calve in the bay, from September to December. A 'whale crier' alerts visitors to their presence with blasts on his seaweed horn. If you're lucky you may see whales within a couple of metres of the Old Harbour wall, but binoculars are advisable. A good vantage point is the scenic path running along the cliffs.

✚ 28A1
🛈 Tourist information
✉ Cnr Lord Mitchell and Lord Roberts ☎ 028-312 2629; fax: 028-313 0305; e-mail: infoburo@hermanus.co.za
🕒 Mon–Sat 9–5; public holidays 10–3. Closed 1 Jan, Easter, 25 Dec

MONTAGU HOT SPRINGS ✪
The small town of Montagu, founded in 1851, is reached via a pass cut through wonderfully contorted strata of red stone. The hot springs for which the town is best known may be visited just for the day or as part of a longer stay at the adjoining hotel and chalets. While in the area visit the wine farms in the Robertson district, and the amazing cactus nursery near Ashton.

✚ 28B1
❓ Hot springs and Avalon Springs Hotel 🕒 Daily 8–5 ☎ 023-614 1150
🛈 Tourist Information ☎ 023-614 2471 (also fax) or 023-614 1116; e-mail: montour@lando.co.za

OUDTSHOORN AND CANGO CAVES ✪✪✪
Oudtshoorn boomed between 1880 and 1914 when the ostrich feathers it produced were in huge demand. More recently it has rebuilt its fortunes through the export of ostrich meat and skins, and through tourism. In and around the town you can visit the lavish mansions of the ostrich barons, the excellent **C P Nel Museum** showing the history of Oudtshoorn, and ostrich farms which display the whole life cycle of the birds.

Thirty kilometres from Oudtshoorn are the spectacular **Cango Caves**, with their huge hall-like caverns, massive limestone stalactites and dramatic dripstone formations. The cave system extends 2km into the hills.

✚ 28C1
🛈 Outdtshoorn Tourist Information ✉ Baron Van Rheede Street ☎ 044-279 2532; fax: 044-272 8226; e-mail: otb@mweb.co.za 🕒 8–6

C P Nel Museum
✉ 3 Baron Van Rheede Street
☎ 044-272 7306 (also fax); e-mail: cpnmuseum@pixie.co.za
🕒 Mon–Fri 8–5; Sat 9–4
💷 Cheap
♿ None

Cango Caves
☎ 044-272 7410
🕒 9–4
🍴 Restaurant (££)
♿ Few
💷 Moderate

Ostriches racing, with and without a jockey, at Oudtshoorn

28A1
Tourist Information
- ✉ 36 Market Street
- ☎ 021-883 9633; e-mail: eikestad@iafrica.com
- 🕐 Mon–Sat 9–5; Sun 10–4

Oom Samie Se Winkel
- ✉ 84 Dorp Street
- ☎ 021-887 0797
- 🕐 Mon–Fri 8:30–5:30, Sat–Sun 9–5

28B1
Tourist Information
- ✉ Oefenrys Huis, Voortrek Street ☎ 028-514 2770 (also fax); e-mail: infoswd@sdn.doria.co.za
- 🕐 Mon–Fri 8–1 and 2–5; Sat 9–12

28A1
Tourist Information
- ✉ 14 Kerk Street
- ☎ 023-230 1348 (also fax) 🕐 Mon–Fri 9–5; Sat 10–1; Sun 11–1:30

Oude Drostdy
- ✉ Main Road (about 4km on Winterhoek Road)
- ☎ 023-230 0203 (also fax)
- 🕐 Mon–Fri 10–12:50, 2–4:50; Sat 10–2; Sun 10–12:50
- ♿ None
- 💲 Free
- ❓ Free wine-tasting

Customers relaxing outside Oom Samie Se Winkel in Stellenbosch

STELLENBOSCH ✪✪✪

Founded in 1679, this oak tree-filled town is home to Stellenbosch University and many other educational institutions, and is the centre of the Western Cape wine industry. Visitors come to see the wine farms in the surrounding countryside and the town's many museums and beautiful thatched and whitewashed Cape Dutch buildings. Take a walk along Dorp Street to see some of the best examples, stopping off at **Oom Samie Se Winkel**, a fascinating shop that's an attraction in its own right. The drive from Stellenbosch over the mountains to the Franschhoek valley takes you over the spectacular Helshoogte Pass and through oak groves and wine farms.

SWELLENDAM ✪✪

Situated below the Langeberg Mountains among shady oaks, the town of Swellendam, founded in 1745, has many fine Cape Dutch and Victorian houses. Swellendam's most striking building is the unusually ornate Dutch Reformed church. The old *drostdy* (house and office of the *landdrost*, or magistrate), dating from 1747 and one of the best examples of such buildings, houses the Drostdy Museum, with its fine display of 18th- and 19th-century furniture.

TULBAGH ✪

Tulbagh was almost destroyed by an earthquake in 1969, but has been painstakingly restored to its 18th-century appearance. The town's buildings constitute its main attraction, in particular the **Oude Drostdy**, now a museum. Also worth a visit is the Oude Kerk Volksmuseum, with displays on the life and material culture of a small Cape country town, and on the 1969 earthquake.

What to See in the Eastern Cape

ADDO ELEPHANT NATIONAL PARK ✪✪✪

The distinctive Addo (from the Khoikhoi word *Gadouw*, meaning river crossing) elephant, with its small tusks, reddish colour and rounded ears, had been hunted almost to extinction when this 100,000ha area was proclaimed a national park in 1931. All that saved it was the dense, impenetrable Addo thorn scrub. Today the number of elephants has risen to over 260, and they have been joined by black rhino, Cape buffalo, eland, red hartebeest, kudu, bushbuck and other species. Visitors must be careful not to run over one of the park's smallest inhabitants, the flightless dung beetle. After rain these insects can be seen in large numbers rolling away rounded dung balls to be used as food and hatcheries for their eggs. Two walking trails can be booked in the park.

🚩 29D1
☎ 012-428 9111; e-mail: reservations@parks-sa.co.za
♿ Good, phone in advance
🎫 Moderate

EAST LONDON ✪

Situated on the Buffalo River, East London gained its present name in 1847, having been known previously as Port Rex. The city has two of the best surfing beaches in the country, Eastern Beach and Nahoon Beach. Its main cultural attractions are the **East London Museum** and the **Ann Bryant Art Gallery**. The former contains an extensive natural history display, including the world's only dodo egg and a stuffed coelacanth. (The first specimen of this fish, thought to have been extinct for 65 million years, was caught off East London in 1938 and brought to the museum.) In the art gallery, works by British and South African artists of the late 19th century onwards are displayed.

🚩 20E2

East London Museum
✉ 319 Oxford Street
☎ 043-743 0686
🕐 Mon–Fri 9:30–5, Sat 2–5, Sun 11:30–4
♿ Excellent
🎫 Cheap

Ann Bryant Art Gallery
✉ 9 St Marks Road, Southern Wood
☎ 043-722 4044
🕐 Mon–Fri 9–5, Sat 9–12
♿ None
🎫 Free

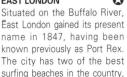

Above: *Latimer's Landing on the East London waterfront*
Right: *the coelacanth, a living fossil*

+ 29D2

i Graaff-Reinet Tourist
Information ☎ 049-
892-4248 (also fax)

Reinet House

✉ Murray Street
☎ 049-892 3801
🕓 Mon–Fri
8–12:30, 2–5, Sat 9–3
♿ None 💷 Cheap

Owl House

✉ Nuwe Straat (street)
☎ 049-841 1733
🕓 Daily 9–5
♿ Good 💷 Cheap

+ 29E1

i Tourist Information ✉
63 High Street ☎ 046-
622 3241; fax: 046-622
3266; e-mail:
info@grahamstown.co.za
🕓 Mon–Fri 8:30–5; Sat
9–1

Albany Museum

✉ Somerset Street
☎ 046-622 2312; fax: 046-
622 2398; e-mail:
l.webley@ru.ac.za
🕓 Tue–Fri 9:30–1, 2–5, Sat
10–2
♿ None
💷 Cheap

Observatory Museum

✉ Bathurst Street
☎ 046-622 2312; fax: 046-
622 2398; e-mail:
l.webley@ru.ac.za
🕓 Tue–Fri 9:30–1, 2-5, Sat
10–2
♿ None
💷 Cheap

+ 29E2

i Tourist Information ☎
045-962 1159

Top: Serpant's Kiss
*sculpture at the Owl
House*
Above: *Grahamstown's
Anglican cathedral*

46

GRAAFF-REINET AND NIEU BETHESDA ✪✪

Known as the 'gem of the Karoo', Graaff-Reinet is a
treasure house of 19th-century Cape Dutch architecture.
More than 200 of the town's buildings have been
declared national monuments. **Reinet House**,
formerly the home of the Dutch Reformed minister
Andrew Murray, is now a historical museum. You can
get some idea of how slaves used to live by visiting
the complex of small houses known as Stretch's Court.
Nieu Bethesda, 50km to the north, is a quiet, pleasant
little Karoo town. Visitors come here to see the weird
Owl House, home of artist Helen Martins. It is filled
with her murals of multicoloured ground glass and
disturbing concrete sculptures of owls and camels,
mermaids and nativity scenes.

GRAHAMSTOWN ✪✪

Grahamstown, founded in 1812 as a military settlement
during the ongoing wars between the British and the
Xhosa, is best known for its many churches and educational institutions, and for its hugely successful annual arts
festival (➤ 116). The town's most imposing building is the
large Anglican Cathedral of St Michael and St George,
dating back to 1824. The **Albany Museum** gives a good
idea of the culture of the indigenous Xhosa, and of the
British settlers who came here in 1820, while the
Observatory Museum houses a working camera obscura.

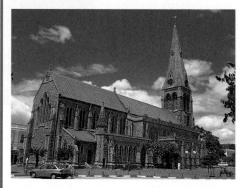

HOGSBACK ✪

Hogsback is a favourite holiday resort for the city-dwellers
of the Eastern Cape. Situated in the Amatola Mountains, it
offers trout fishing and walks through virgin indigenous
forest. At 1,200–1,300m above sea level the area is cool in
summer and often blanketed in snow during the winter.
The Arboretum, a living museum of trees, contains many
indigenous species such as yellowwoods, white ironwood
and assegaai-wood, as well as exotics such as California
redwoods and holy cypresses.

MOUNTAIN ZEBRA NATIONAL PARK ✪✪

Occupying some 6,500ha of mountainous Karoo landscape, this park was originally created to accommodate the nearly extinct mountain zebra (*Equus zebra*). This species, of which there are now over 200 in the park, is distinguished from the much more common Burchell's zebra (*Equus burchelli*) by its thinner stripes and mane, and its distinctive dewlap. Many other animals, including 200 species of bird, the caracal wild cat and a variety of antelope, share the park with the zebra. A three-day hiking trail is available; phone the park.

PORT ELIZABETH ✪

The Governor of the Cape, Sir Rufane Donkin, named this port in honour of his wife Elizabeth after she died, commemorating her by a small stone pyramid in the Donkin Reserve, in front of the Lighthouse. The chief attractions of the city are its well-known **Oceanarium** with seal and dolphin shows, the Snake Park, the 56m-high Campanile Clock Tower housing a carillon of 23 bells, and the Port Elizabeth Museum.

About 50km south of the town are two of the world's finest surfing beaches, at St Francis Bay and Jeffreys Bay.

WILD COAST ✪✪

This stretch of the Eastern Cape coast is one of the most scenic yet least visited parts of South Africa. There are reasons for this: the roads from the N2 down to the tiny coastal resorts are often extremely bad, and the area can be dangerous. But it is well worth the effort to visit places such as Qora Mouth, Mazeppa Bay, Coffee Bay and the larger town of Port St Johns. You will find deserted beaches, wide river mouths, mountainous sand dunes, stretches of virgin coastal forest – and delicious seafood.

🚩 29D2
☎ 012-428 9111; e-mail: reservations@parks-sa.co.za
♿ Good, but phone in advance
💷 Moderate

🚩 29D1
ℹ Tourist Information ☎ 041-585 8884; e-mail: information@tourismpe.co.za

Oceanarium
✉ Beach Road, Humewood
☎ 041-584 0650
🕐 9–4:30 🍴 Café (£)
♿ Few 💷 Moderate

🚩 29F2
ℹ Tourist Information ☎ 047-531 5290; fax: 047 531 5291

Above: *dolphins at Port Elizabeth Oceanarium*

47

Northeast Region

This region includes a variety of landscapes: hundreds of kilometres of subtropical coastline, the rolling hills of the KwaZulu-Natal Midlands, the Drakensberg and Soutpansberg mountains, and the open savannah of eastern Mpumalanga. The diversity of the landscape is matched by the diversity of its peoples: Zulu, Ndebele, Venda, Tsonga, English- and Afrikaans-speaking whites, and a sizeable Indian population, mainly in KwaZulu-Natal. The chief urban centres are Durban, Pietermaritzburg, Nelspruit and Pholokwane (formerly Pietersburg).

The glory of the region is its outstanding national parks. Visitors flock to the Kruger National Park in the hope of seeing Africa's Big Five, and to the Blyde River Canyon for its breathtaking views. Black and white rhino are the main attraction of the Hluhluwe-Umfolozi park, while hippo, pelican and flamingo draw nature-lovers to the Greater St Lucia Wetland, declared a World Heritage Site in 1999.

> *'The scenery throughout from Durban to Pieter Maritzburg is interesting and in some places is very beautiful.'*
>
> ANTHONY TROLLOPE,
> *South Africa* (1878)

---•---

A reminder of war in front of the Durban City Hall

Durban

Durban's fine beaches and many hotels make it South Africa's premier holiday resort. This city, named in 1835 after the Governor of the Cape, Sir Benjamin D'Urban, is one of the fastest-growing urban conglomerations in the world. Like most urban centres in South Africa, it is a mixture of downtown skyscrapers and neat middle-class suburbs, with sprawling townships and shacklands around the perimeter. With its superb natural harbour, it has long been the country's largest, busiest port.

Although Durban can be uncomfortably hot and humid in midsummer, for most of the year it enjoys wonderfully mild, sunny weather. The city is very much geared to low- and middle-income tourism, with many activities for families and fun-lovers along the beachfront. Watersports, fishing, golf, shops, restaurants, rickshaw rides, snake parks – Durban has them all.

Above: *Durban rickshaw man and his vehicle*
Below: *shopping for African art*
Below right: *magnificent lily pads in the Botanic Gardens*

What to See in Durban

AFRICAN ARTS CENTRE ✪

This centre, run on a non-profit basis, is an excellent place to buy traditional African art from the townships around the city, the long-established arts centre at Rorke's Drift and all parts of KwaZulu-Natal. Here you can find many kinds of beadwork, woven baskets, pottery, textiles, woodcarvings and wire sculptures. The centre also provides information about other African art outlets in the area.

 54B1
✉ 1st Floor, Tourist Junction, Old Street Building, 160 Pine Street
☎ 031-304 7915 (also fax); email afriart1@iafrica.com
🕐 Mon–Fri 8:30–5, Sat 9–1
♿ None
💷 Free

BOTANIC GARDENS ✪✪

An ivory hunter named John Cane originally owned the land on which these gardens were laid out in 1848. They contain beautiful stands of striped green and yellow bamboo, old cycads (palms), fine established trees and a scent garden for the blind. One of the highlights is the collection of orchids.

 54B1
✉ 70 St Thomas Road
☎ 031-201 1303
🕐 7:30–5:45
🍴 Snack bar (£)
♿ Good
💷 Free

CITY HALL AND MUSEUMS ★★

Belfast in Northern Ireland provided the model for Durban's elaborate City Hall, built in 1910. The result is an interesting example of colonial baroque, set amid graceful palm trees. Within the same building and city block are several museums and galleries. The **Durban Art Gallery** has a good collection of Victorian painting, contemporary South African art, Chinese ceramics and Lalique glass from France. In the **Natural Science Museum** you can see extensive realistic displays of stuffed birds, reptiles, fishes and insects, as well as a dodo skeleton and an ancient Egyptian mummy. The nearby **Old Court House Museum** houses fascinating displays relating to the social, economic and political history of Durban.

✝ 54B1

Art Gallery & Museums
⊠ City Hall, West Street
☎ 031-311 2265 (Art Gallery); 031-311 2250 (Natural Science Museum); 031-311 2297 (Old Court House Museum)
🕐 Mon–Sat 8–4, Sun 11–4
🍴 Café in Natural Science Museum (£)
♿ None
💷 Free

GOLDEN MILE ★

This stretch of the Durban beachfront between Addington Beach to the south and Blue Lagoon to the north is the heart of the city's tourist area. Many hotels and blocks of holiday apartments line the strip. Sightseers stroll up and down the promenade, swimmers enjoy a dip in the warm Indian Ocean and surfers ride the well-formed waves, while sun-worshippers soak up the rays. On the Golden Mile you can take a rickshaw ride, visit the funfair or buy African art from pavement vendors. But be on your guard: many petty thieves and pickpockets operate here.

✝ 54B1
⊠ Marine Parade
ℹ Tourist Information
  ⊠ 160 Pine Street
  ☎ 031-304 4934;
  🕐 Mon–Fri 8–4:30; Sat 9–2

KILLIE CAMPBELL COLLECTIONS ★★

Muckleneuk, the mansion built by the sugar baron Sir Marshall Campbell, is home to the Killie Campbell Museum, known for its fine collections of Africana. Campbell's daughter, Margaret Roach (Killie) Campbell, collected prints, artefacts, pictures, books and maps relating to Africa, particularly Natal and its tribes, and these now form the core of the museum. Noteworthy are the several hundred paintings of tribal dress by local artist Barbara Tyrrell, and the displays of Zulu beadwork. The gardens around the house are particularly beautiful, landscaped in Victorian style.

✝ 54B1
⊠ 220 Marriott Road
☎ 031-207 3711; fax 031-209 1622
🕐 By appointment (Jenny Harkness 031-207 34342, Mon–Fri 8:30–4:30)
♿ None
💷 Moderate

African art in the Killie Campbell Collection

54B1
130 Ordinance Road
031-311 2223; e-mail:
lynnec@prcsu.durban.
gov.za
Mon–Sat 8–4, Sun 11–4
Good
Free

54B1
2 West Street
031-337 3536
Daily 9–5. Shows 10:15,
11:45, 2:30; shark-
feeding 12:30; fish-
feeding 11, 3:30
Few
Expensive

54B1

Hindu Temple
890 Bellair Road
031-261 8114
Daily 6–6
Few
Free

KWAMUHLE MUSEUM ✪

The name KwaMuhle ('place of the good one') commemorates J S Marwick, an official who helped thousands of Zulus return to their homes from the Transvaal during the Anglo-Boer War. The museum occupies the former offices of the Bantu Administration Board. Its fascinating displays show the social history of South African cities, Durban in particular, from the perspective of the black majority.

SEAWORLD AND DOLPHINARIUM ✪✪

This is one of the finest aquariums in the country. On display here are most of the species of sharks found in KwaZulu-Natal waters (swimmers needn't worry – all the province's main swimming beaches are fully protected by shark nets). If you arrive at the right time you can watch the sharks being fed by divers. There are also turtles and many kinds of tropical fish. The adjacent dolphinarium puts on shows starring dolphins, penguins and seals.

SRI AMBALAVANAR HINDU TEMPLE ✪

This colourful temple on Bellair Road, 3km west of the city centre, is the site of a fire-walking ceremony held each Easter and attended by thousands, both Hindu and non-Hindu. All are welcome to attempt the barefoot crossing of the pits filled with glowing embers. The temple is just one sign of the substantial Indian presence in Durban. From 1860 to 1911 some 152,000 Indians came to KwaZulu-Natal, most to work as indentured labourers in the sugar-cane plantations, often under appalling conditions. Among the immigrants was Gandhi (▶ 11).

The area around Grey Street, in the city centre, is the heart of the Indian business district. The shops here, selling a range of spices and curry powders, imported Indian brasswork and brightly coloured textiles, are well worth a visit.

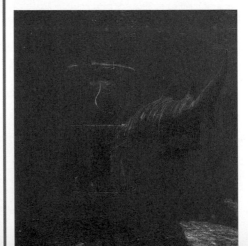

Shark-feeding time at Durban's Seaworld

Valley of a Thousand Hills

This drive takes you through the scenic hill country west of Durban, dotted with traditional Zulu homesteads.

Light and shadow over the Valley of a Thousand Hills

Take the N3 out of Durban in the direction of Pietermaritzburg, then the M13 towards Pinetown and Kloof. Just after Kloof take the turn-off on to the R103 in the direction of Hillcrest. You are now on a stretch of the Old Main Road from Durban to Pietermaritzburg. Continue on to Botha's Hill.

At Botha's Hill there are excellent views over the Valley of a Thousand Hills. You can also visit **Phezulu Safari Park**, a re-creation of a Zulu village, with traditional Zulu dancing and a craft centre.

Continue on the R103 for 5km and turn right to the Rob Roy Hotel.

Have lunch or tea at the hotel, a strange European fantasy in the middle of rural KwaZulu-Natal. Outstanding viewpoints can be found at the hotel and about 700m past it on the same road.

Return to the R103 and drive to Drummond.

There are wonderful vistas of the Valley of a Thousand Hills from the town and from around it. As you drive the R103 spare a thought for the athletes who run this way each year in the Comrades Marathon between Durban and Pietermaritzburg.

The R103 winds on through Inchanga and Cato Ridge. At Camperdown turn on to the N3 and return to Durban on the highway.

This route takes you through attractive low hills and grassland back into the city.

Distance
120km

Time
1½ hours without stops,
4 hours with stops

Start/end point
Durban city centre
 54B1

Lunch or tea
Rob Roy Hotel (£–££)
☎ 031-777-1305

Phezulu Safari Park
✉ 5 Old Main Road, Botha's Hill
☎ 031-777 1000
🕐 Daily 8:30–5

53

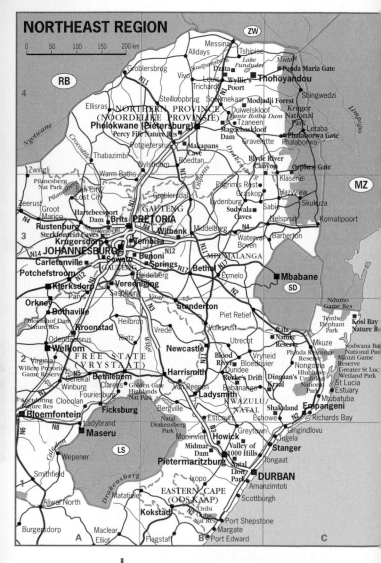

NORTHEAST REGION

What to See in KwaZulu-Natal

DUNDEE AND LADYSMITH BATTLEGROUNDS 😊😊

Some of the most famous battles in South African history between Afrikaner and Zulu, Zulu and Briton, and Briton and Afrikaner, were fought on KwaZulu-Natal territory. In the region around Dundee you can visit Isandlwana Historic Reserve, where Zulu warriors inflicted a heavy defeat on the British army during the Anglo-Zulu War of 1879, and Rorke's Drift, where the British repulsed a strong Zulu attack. Also in this area is Blood River. Here 64 bronze ox-wagons mark the place where a Boer commando of 464 men and 64 wagons, led by Andries Pretorius, defeated a Zulu force of 3,000 in 1838.

In and around Ladysmith are many memorials to the Anglo-Boer War. **Ladysmith Siege Museum** has displays relating to the siege of the British in the town by the Boers, which lasted for nearly four months from 1899 into 1900. Notable Anglo-Boer War sites near by include Wagon Hill, 5km south of Ladysmith, and Spioenkop, off the R60, west of town.

DRAKENSBERG (► 18, TOP TEN)

✚	54B2
ℹ	Dundee Tourist Information ✉ Victoria Street 🕐 Mon–Fri 9–4:45; Sat 9–12 ☎ 034-212 2121; fax: 034-218 2837; e-mail: tourism@dundeekzn.co.za
ℹ	Ladysmith Tourist Information ☎ 036-637 2992 (also fax); e-mail: info@ladysmith.co.za

Ladysmith Siege Museum
✉ Murchison Street, Ladysmith
☎ 036-637 2992 (also fax)
🕐 Mon–Fri 9–4; Sat 9–1

Rorke's Drift, where Zulu and Briton clashed in 1879

GREATER ST LUCIA WETLAND PARK 😊😊😊

Covering some 38,700ha, this park was declared a World Heritage Site in 1999 in recognition of its unique importance. Surrounding the St Lucia Lake are a variety of distinct ecosystems including estuarine, wetland, mangrove swamp, coastal dune, virgin marine and coastal forest. Highlights of the park are its numerous hippos and crocodiles, and its abundant bird life, especially flamingoes and pelicans. You can take boat rides, go on game drives and enjoy the rich fishing.

✚	54C2
☎	033-845 1000; book at www.kznwildlife.com
ℹ	Area Tourist Information ☎ (cell) 082-870 7072
♿	Few

54C2

☎ 033-845 1000; book at
www.kznwildlife.com

🕐 Mon–Fri 7–5, Sat 7–3

♿ Good, but phone in
advance

✋ Moderate

HLUHLUWE-UMFOLOZI NATIONAL PARK ✪✪✪

Hluhluwe and Umfolozi, originally separate parks, have
been joined together by an 8km-wide corridor to create a
single reserve of 96,000ha. The park encompasses many
habitats – thick scrub, grassland, forest, savannah and
woodland – which in turn support a wide range of animals.
Most famous are the numerous white rhinos, bred here
from the point of near extinction. They share the park with
black rhinos, the rest of the Big Five (➤ 6), antelope,
zebra, warthog, hippo and hundreds of species of bird. You
can book walking trails through the park.

54B1

ℹ Pietermaritzburg Tourist
Information ✉ 77
Commercial Road ☎
033-345 1348 🕐
Mon–Fri 8–5; Sat 8–3;
Sun 9–3. Midlands
Meander Information
☎ 033-330 8195

PIETERMARITZBURG AND THE MIDLANDS ✪✪

Named after the two Voortrekker leaders, Piet Retief and
Gert Maritz, Pietermaritzburg became the capital of the
Colony of Natal after the British occupation of 1838.
'Maritzburg (as it is known) still retains a strongly British
colonial feel, and has rightly been called the best preserved
Victorian city in the world. A stroll through the area around
Church Street will take you past the magnificent red-brick
City Hall, the historic Supreme Court and the Legislative
Assembly Building of 1889. The strong presence of India
and Islam is represented by the Top Mosque, just off
upper Church Street, and the Sri Siva Soobramoniar and
Marriamen Temple on the corner of Williams and lower
Longmarket streets.

From Pietermaritzburg you have easy access to the
green foothills of the Drakensberg known as the Midlands.
Picnic at Midmar Dam, view the 95m-high Howick Falls or
take the 'Midlands Meander' from Hilton to Hidcote,
visiting arts and crafts studios and antiques shops.

Below: *impala by the
water in the Hluhluwe-
Umfolozi National Park*
Inset: *the graceful
cascade of Howick Falls*

PORT SHEPSTONE AND THE SOUTH COAST ✪

The chain of seaside resorts strung out along the coast south of Durban is one of South Africa's most popular holiday areas. From Port Shepstone you can take the Banana Express on a narrow-gauge railway through banana and sugar-cane plantations. Near by is the spectacular 24km-long Oribi Gorge, with scenic drives and hiking trails. Attractions at the resort of Scottburgh include Croc World and a miniature railway. The small town of Shelly Beach, just south of Port Shepstone, has a Shell Museum with a magnificent collection of specimens.

TONGAAT AND THE NORTH COAST ✪

Though less built-up than the South Coast, the coast north of Durban also has several very popular holiday resorts. Umhlanga Rocks offers large tourist hotels, seafood restaurants and the nearby **Natal Sharks Board**, where a daily audio-visual presentation on sharks is followed by the dissection of a shark.

In the mainly Indian town of Tongaat you can visit the country's oldest Hindu place of worship, the Juggernath Puri Temple, learn about the sugar industry at Hulett's Maidstone Mill, or see crocodiles at Crocodile Creek.

All along the coast are excellent beaches and there is a good chance of seeing schools of dolphins.

ZULULAND ✪

The town of Eshowe is a good base for exploring the kingdom of Zululand, which reached the height of its power under Shaka in the early 19th century. The **Vukani Museum** and the Zululand Historical Museum, with their displays of arts, crafts and furniture, give a good insight into Zulu culture.

Re-creations of Zulu settlements can be seen at **Shakaland**, 14km from Eshowe, originally the set for the TV series *Shaka Zulu*, and at other cultural villages near by.

🚩 54B1
ℹ️ Port Shepstone Tourist Information ✉️ Princess Elizabeth Drive ☎ 039-682 2455. South Coast Tourist Information ✉️ Panorama Parade, Margate Beachfront ☎ 039-312 2322. 🕐 Mon–Fri 8–4:30; Sat 9–11

🚩 54B1

ℹ️ Tongaat Tourist (Sugar Coast) Information ☎ 031-561 4257

Natal Sharks Board
☎ 14 Herrwood Drive, Umhlanga Rocks
☎ 031-566 0400; www.shark.co.za
🕐 Tue, Wed Thu at 9 and 2; Sun at 2

🚩 54C2
ℹ️ Eshowe Tourist Information ✉️ Osbourne Road ☎ 035-474 1141 🕐 Mon–Fri 7:30–4

Vukani Museum
✉️ Osbourne Street, Eshowe
☎ 035-474 5274; e-mail: cordic@intekom.co.za

Shakaland
✉️ Off the R66 between Eshowe and Melmoth
☎ 035-460 0912; e-mail: res@shakaland.com
🕐 Mon–Fri 6AM–9PM

A young Zulu warrior dancing

In the Know

If you only have a short time to visit South Africa, or would like to get a real flavour of the country, here are some ideas:

Ways to Be a Local

Use the 3-stage handshake. Shake hands in the Western way, clasp hands with thumbs on top, then repeat stage one.

Call things *lekker*. This all-purpose word (Afrikaans for 'nice') can be applied to anything, from a meal to a fine sunset.

Walk around in shorts in all weather, in the city or on the beach.

Praise South African sports teams – the locals will love it.

Travel by minibus-taxi, as millions of South Africans do (but leave your valuables at home!)

Raise a laugh by greeting people with the colloquial 'Hello, howzit' – to which the response may be 'Ja well no fine'.

Talk to people. Most South Africans love to chat.

Try unusual foods such as prickly-pear fruit, maize meal and, if you're really daring, mopani worms.

Mix in with your English any words of Afrikaans, Sotho, Zulu or Xhosa that you may have picked up.

Refer to Nelson Mandela as Madiba. Many South Africans use Mandela's clan praise-name, Madiba, as an affectionate and respectful way of naming him.

Good Places to Have Lunch

Vineyard Hotel (£–££) ✉
Colinton Road, Newlands, Cape Town ☎ 021-683 3044. Hotel with a choice of restaurants. Superb views from the garden.

Mount Nelson (£££) ✉
76 Orange Street, Cape Town ☎ 021-483 1000. Famous luxury hotel with three fine restaurants.

The Wild Fig (££) ✉
Courtyard Hotel complex, Liesbeeck Avenue, Mowbray, Cape Town ☎ 021-448 0507. Housed in an 18th-century barn, this restaurant offers a blend of Thai, South African and Greek specialties.

Cock House (££) ✉ 10 Market Street, Grahamstown ☎ 046-636 1287. Restaurant and guest house in a National Monument.

Star of the West (££) ✉
Corner of Barkly and North Circular roads, Kimberley ☎ 053-832 6463.

Mopani worms, a local delicacy

Atmospheric restored 19th-century miners' pub.

Baccarat (£££) ✉
Admiral's Court, Mutual Gardens, Rosebank, Johannesburg ☎ 011-880 1835. French-Huguenot style buffet; specialities include bouillabaisse, kudu, trout and other fish dishes.

Coachman's Inn (££) ✉
29 Peter Place, Lyme Park, Sandton, Johannesburg ☎ 011-706 7269. Wide-ranging, international food of consistently good quality.

Legends Café (£–££) ✉
Musgrave Centre, Musgrave Road, Durban ☎ 031-201 0733. Serves a range of light meals at affordable prices.

Langoustine-by-the-Sea (££) ✉ 131 Waterkant Street, Durban North ☎ 031-563 7324. Good seafood with sea views.

Café Riche (£–££) ✉
2 Church Square, Pretoria ☎ 012-328 3173. Oldest café in Pretoria. Light lunches, dish-of-the-day.

Top Activities

Take a hot bath. South Africa has many natural hot springs, which are great places to visit in winter. If you're the indoor type, try a steam bath at Cape Town's Long Street Baths (➤ 35).

Go to a sporting event. In sports-mad South Africa this is a must. Watch soccer, the country's most

popular sport, at Johannesburg's FNB Stadium; enjoy rugby at Durban's Kings Park; or take in a cricket match at the loveliest ground anywhere, Newlands in Cape Town.

Try an adventure activity. Mountain-biking through superb countryside, hot-air ballooning over Gauteng, bungee jumping, paragliding, scuba diving, whitewater rafting and sea-kayaking are available.

Visit a session of Parliament (➤ 35). Watch the country's new democracy in action. The opening of Parliament in Cape Town in February has become a showcase of South African dress styles, from ethnic African to Voortrekker chic.

Stroll through botanical gardens. Two of the loveliest and the most restful locales in South Africa are Cape Town's Kirstenbosch (➤ 42) and Durban's Botanic Gardens (➤ 50).

Riding the waves in style off Durban's North Beach

Muizenberg, Cape Town. Popular swimming and surfing beach.

Plettenberg Bay, Garden Route (➤ 19). Some of the best golden, sandy beaches in South Africa.

Nahoon Beach, East London (➤ 45). Outstanding surfing beach.

North Beach, Durban. The most popular and populous beach in the country.

Above: *Newlands Cricket Ground and, below, white rhino in the Hluhluwe-Umfolozi National Park*

10
Top Nature Reserves

- **Addo Elephant National Park** (➤ 45).
- **Augrabies Falls National Park** (➤ 85).
- **Blyde River Canyon Nature Reserve** (➤ 16).
- **Golden Gate Highlands National Park** (➤ 20).
- **Greater St Lucia Wetland Park** (➤ 55).
- **Hluhluwe-Umfolozi National Park** (➤ 56).
- **Kgalagadi Transfrontier Park** (➤ 85).
- **Kruger National Park** (➤ 22–23).
- **Mountain Zebra National Park** (➤ 47).
- **Pilanesberg National Park** (➤ 87).

5
Top Beaches

Clifton, Cape Town. Very fashionable sunbathing spot, with dazzlingly white sands.

➕ 54C3
ℹ️ Tourist Office ☎ 013-712 5055; fax: 013-712 2885 🕐 Mon–Fri 8:30–5; Sat, Sun 9–3

Barberton Museum
✉️ 36 Pilgrim Street
☎ 013-712 4208 (also fax)
🕐 Daily 9–4
♿ Good
👆 Free
❓ Phone for details of tours of historic houses

Below: *mature cycads in the Modjadji Forest and, inset, workers in the tea plantations at Magoebaskloof*

➕ 54B4
ℹ️ Tzaneen Tourist Office
✉️ 25 Danie Joubert Street ☎ 015-307 1294; fax: 015-307 2123 🕐 Mon–Fri 8–5; Sat 8–11

What to See in Mpumalanga and Northern Province

BARBERTON ⭐⭐

Cockney Liz and Florrie the Golden Dane were just two of the 'good-time girls' attracted to this place when gold was discovered here in 1884. Barberton, named after the Barber cousins who found the main ore-bearing reef, expanded into a warren of bars, gambling halls, canteens and stock exchanges in just two years, but the town collapsed when the miners moved to the richer diggings of the Witwatersrand. A number of buildings from the boom days have been preserved, including the Transvaal's first Stock Exchange, the 1887 Globe Tavern, Belhaven House and Stopforth House (1886). **Barberton Museum** highlights the gold rush and the geology of the area. In front of the town hall a lifesize statue of Jock of the Bushveld, a Staffordshire bull terrier, commemorates the hero of Percy Fitzpatrick's famous novel of the same name.

BLYDE RIVER CANYON (▶ 16, TOP TEN)

KRUGER NATIONAL PARK (▶ 22–23, TOP TEN)

LETABA DISTRICT ⭐

This district, around the town of Tzaneen, has several attractive spots to visit. The Modjadji Forest is home to a spectacular grove of cycads, strange primitive plants unchanged in form for millions of years. These mature plants have survived because they are sacred to the famed 16th-century Rain Queen, said to have been the inspiration for Rider Haggard's novel *She*.

A short drive from Tzaneen will take you through tea estates, eucalyptus plantations and indigenous forest to Magoebaskloof Dam and the Debengeni Falls. Another popular resort in the area is the Fanie Botha Dam.

Historic Pilgrim's Rest

This walk takes you through the historic centre of the delightful old mining town of Pilgrim's Rest (➤ 62).

Start where the road from Sabie enters the town's main street. You will see a succession of historic buildings on your left.

First is the small Anglican Church of St Mary, made of brick. Next comes the corrugated-iron Town Hall, followed by Leadley's Building. If you look towards the creek on your right, you will see some of the old alluvial diggings. From here on in quick succession are: the Old Print House, now a shop; the Pilgrim's and Sabie News; and the European Hotel.

At this point bear right along the curving stretch of road leading to the Tourist Information Centre.

On your right is a house with a wide veranda. This is Chaitow, named after its former owner, the jack-of-all-trades C H Chaitow. Next on the right is the Information Centre, where you can buy a ticket giving admission to all the town's museums. The Royal Hotel, opposite, has displays of old mining gear.

Walk on past the Information Centre, continuing to bear right.

The old Post Office on the left is now a museum. Opposite, to the right, is the Miner's House Museum, which demonstrates the lifestyle of a miner in the 1910s, with furniture made from old dynamite boxes.

Reminders of the old mining days in Pilgrim's Rest

If you have the time, get a map from the Information Centre and take the longer walk to see the historic Cemetery, the Central Reduction Works and the stone-built Joubert Bridge.

Distance
2km

Time
1 hour without stops, 3 hours with stops

Start point
Where the Sabie road enters Pilgrim's Rest
➕ 54B3

End point
Miner's House Museum
➕ 54B3

Lunch or tea
Scott's Café (££)
☎ 013-768 1061

54B3
Tourist Office ☎ 013-768 1060; fax: 013-768 1469

54B3
✉ About 35km northwest of Nelspruit, off the R539
☎ 013-733 4152; fax: 013-733 5266;
www.soft.co.za/dinopark
🕐 Daily 8:30–4:30
🍴 Restaurant (££), café (£)
♿ Few
📷 Moderate

54B4
Louis Trichardt Tourist Office ☎ 015-516 0040

Washing day at a Venda homestead

PILGRIM'S REST ✪✪

The wood and corrugated-iron buildings of Pilgrim's Rest, a striking survival from the 19th century, show what life was like in a mining camp of the old Transvaal. In 1873, Alec Patterson discovered South Africa's richest deposit of alluvial gold here. Although the focus of mining interest shifted to the Witwatersrand, extraction of gold continued here into the 20th century. Pilgrim's Rest has remained virtually intact and can be viewed on a walking tour (➤ 61).

SUDWALA CAVES ✪

These caves, situated in Mankelekele Mountain, were formed by the action of water percolating through the dolomitic rock. They are named after Sudwala, a Swazi who took refuge here in the 19th century. Only 600m of the vast cave system are open to the public, but guided tours take you through passages into large chambers where fantastic dripstone formations can be seen. On the ceiling are the round shapes of fossilised stromalites, algae which were among the earliest living organisms on earth.

VENDA ✪

The region of the Venda people in the Soutpansberg (Salt Pan Mountains) is famous for its secretive rituals and sacred places. The holiest spot of all is Lake Fundudzi, said to have been the home of a fertility god in the form of a huge python. From the main urban centre of the area, Louis Trichardt, you can take a drive to the Hangklip Forest Reserve or through the scenic pass of Wyllie's Poort.

Swaziland

The 365sq km Kingdom of Swaziland is surrounded on three sides by South Africa, and on the fourth by Mozambique. Culturally, the people belong to the Nguni group, which includes the Xhosa and the Zulu of South Africa. The country is ruled by an absolute monarch, at present King Mswati III. Farming, forestry, mining and the export of labour to South Africa provide most of the country's income.

The capital, Mbabane, lies in a pleasant hilly setting. Don't miss its Swazi market, with fresh produce, woven items and handicrafts on sale. To the southeast is the Ezulwini Valley ('place of heaven'), which has several hotels, hot springs, a casino, Parliament and the Swazi royal residence at Lobamba. Mlilwane Wildlife Sanctuary (5,000ha), also in the valley, is noted for the bird life around its several dams; many other animals which had virtually become extinct in the area are to be found here, including hippo, eland, giraffe and warthog.

Two other reserves can be visited in the more savannah-like eastern part of Swaziland: the Hlane Royal National Park and the rugged Mkhaya Game Reserve, both of which have larger animals, such as elephant and rhino.

Piggs Peak in the mountainous northwest part of Swaziland, once a mining centre, is now a commercial forestry area. The district offers wonderful scenic drives and good hikes.

Swaziland is famous for two colourful annual ceremonies – the women's *Umhlanga* (reed) dance, and the young men's *Ncwala* (first fruits) ceremony.

54C3

Swaziland Tourist Information ☎ 09268-404 4556

Main picture: *reed-bearers in the* Umhlanga *dance*
Below: *Swazi weaver at work*

Gauteng

Just 150 years ago this part of the former Transvaal was home to scattered tribes, farmers, small Voortrekker towns and wild animals. Now Gauteng is the economic powerhouse of South Africa, producing a third of the country's wealth, and though it is by far the smallest province, it has the highest concentration of city-dwellers. The reason for the dramatic change was the discovery of gold on the Witwatersrand (White Water Ridge) in 1886, which brought with it a massive influx of population and the rapid growth of cities.

Today the province is an almost continuous urban-industrial sprawl, from Vereeniging and Vanderbijlpark in the south, and Johannesburg and Soweto in the centre, to Pretoria in the north. For the visitor, the main attractions lie in the art galleries, museums, shops, theatres and restaurants of Johannesburg and Pretoria, and the people and historic interest of Soweto.

> *'Ancient Nineveh and Babylon have been revived. Johannesburg is their twentieth-century prototype.'*
>
> Australian journalist
> (describing Johannesburg in 1910)

Headgear at Crown Mines gold mine, Gold Reef City

Downtown Johannesburg viewed from the top of the Carlton Centre

Johannesburg

Although the seat of government lies elsewhere, Johannesburg is South Africa's largest city and the undisputed economic, industrial and financial capital of the country.

DID YOU KNOW?

South Africa is the world's biggest producer of gold, platinum, diamonds, chrome ore, manganese and vanadium.

Visitors to the Johannesburg Art Gallery

Johannesburg (aka Joburg) is a city built on gold – hence its African name, Egoli, 'place of gold'. An obscure prospector, George Harrison, first discovered the precious metal here in 1886. Within a year a mining town of 10,000 people had sprung up. By 1889 the young city had horse-drawn trams, and by 1890 electric lights. Soon fashionable suburbs appeared, such as Parktown (► 71) with its stone-built mansions. Nine years after the discovery of gold the population of Johannesburg was 100,000; today it is several million. With the mines came many associated industries, commerce, financial institutions and a stock exchange which has grown into the largest in Africa.

Present-day Johannesburg is several cities in one. The original city centre, with its offices and skyscrapers, has the vibrant feel of an African city, with many pavement-vendors from neighbouring countries. Because of the former policy of racial segregation, a separate black city, Soweto, has grown up to the southwest. Many big businesses and the stock exchange have recently moved north to the wealthy area of Sandton, where high-rise buildings are mushrooming.

Because of its wealth, Johannesburg has some of the country's finest and most expensive shops, some of its best museums, theatres and art galleries, and some of its most luxurious homes. But as in other South African cities, wealth exists alongside poverty and deprivation.

What to See in Johannesburg

CARLTON CENTRE ✪

This downtown Johannesburg building, 50 storeys and 200m high, contains shops, offices, restaurants, cinemas and an ice rink, but its most attractive feature is the view from the top floor, the **Top of Africa Panorama**. Go on a smog-free day so that you can enjoy the spectacular view – on a clear day you can see Pretoria, 58km away.

GOLD REEF CITY ✪✪✪

Designed to give visitors the feel of 19th-century gold-mining Johannesburg, this theme park is built around an old mine, Crown Mines No 14 Shaft. You can go more than 200m underground and experience what life was like for the early miners, and there are demonstrations of molten gold being poured to make ingots. Lining the reconstructed Victorian streets are shops, a hotel, a bank, a newspaper office, an antique apothecary's establishment, a laundry and a brewery. The park has fairground rides, and performances by African dance troupes.

JOHANNESBURG ART GALLERY ✪✪

Construction of this gallery, designed by Sir Edwin Lutyens and financed by Johannesburg's gold barons, began in 1911. The moving spirit behind its creation was the wife of one of the Randlords, Lady Philips. In line with the policy of most South African galleries, at first only European art was collected; the gallery owns a fine Rodin sculpture and works by El Greco and Picasso. Later it acquired works by leading South African artists such as Pierneef, Irma Stern, Jackson Hlungwane and William Kentridge. Most recently the Brenthurst Collection of African art (mainly from southern and eastern Africa) has been added.

✚ 69C2

Top of Africa Panorama
✉ Commissioner Street
☎ 011-308 1331
🕐 Mon–Fri 9–7
♿ Good 🎫 Cheap

✚ 68B1
✉ Shaft 14, Northern Park Way, Ormonde
☎ 011-248 6800; fax: 011-248 6863; e-mail: info@goldreefcity.co.za
🕐 Tue–Sun 9:30–5
🍴 Restaurants, pubs, café (£–££)
♿ Good
🎫 Moderate

✚ 69C2
✉ King George Street, Joubert Park
☎ 011-725 3130
🕐 Tue–Sun 10–5
♿ Good, but phone in advance
🎫 Free

Johannesburg's theme park, Gold Reef City

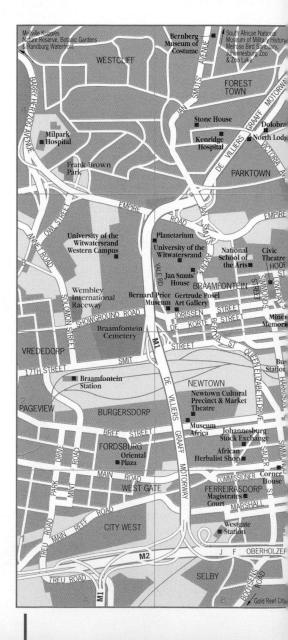

Melville Koppies
Nature Reserve, Botanic Gardens
& Randburg Waterfront

WESTCLIFF

Bernberg
Museum of
Costume

South African National
Museum of Military History
Melrose Bird Sanctuary,
Johannesburg Zoo
& Zoo Lake

FOREST
TOWN

Stone House

Milpark
Hospital

Kenridge
Hospital

Dolobra

North Lodge

Frank Brown
Park

PARKTOWN

EMPIRE

ROAD

EMPIRE

University of the
Witwatersrand
Western Campus

Planetarium

University of the
Witwatersrand

National
School of
the Arts

Civic
Theatre

HOOF
ST

Jan Smuts
House

BRAAMFONTEIN

Wembley
International
Raceway

Bernard Price
Museum

Gertrude Posel
Art Gallery

JORISSEN

STREET

Mine
Memorial

Braamfontein
Cemetery

DE

KORTE

STREET

BERTHA ST

STREET

Bus
Station

VREDEDORP

SMIT

17TH STREET

Braamfontein
Station

NEWTOWN

Newtown Cultural
Precinct & Market
Theatre

PAGEVIEW

BURGERSDORP

Museum
Africa

Johannesburg
Stock Exchange

BREE

STREET

FORDSBURG

African
Herbalist Shop

Oriental
Plaza

MAIN

ROAD

WEST GATE

COMMISSIONER

Corner
House

FERREIRASDORP

Magistrates
Court

MARSHALL

CITY WEST

Westgate
Station

M2

J F OBERHOLZER

SELBY

TREU ROAD

M1

Gold Reef City

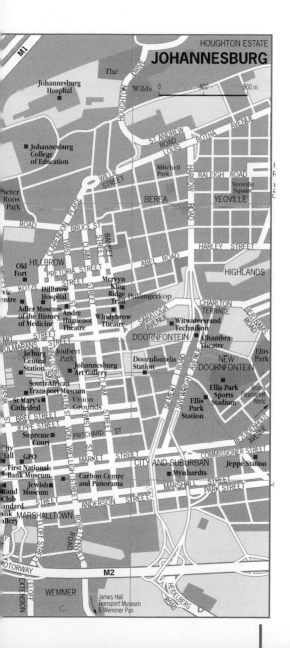

HOUGHTON ESTATE

JOHANNESBURG

The

Wilds

0   400   800 m

M1

Johannesburg
Hospital

ST ANDREW ROAD

LOUIS

BOTHA

AVENUE

Johannesburg
College
of Education

HOUGHTON DRIVE

WILLIE STREET

Mitchell
Park

HARROW ROAD

RALEIGH ROAD

Yeoville
Square

Pieter
Roos
Park

BEREA

YEOVILLE

ROAD

CLARENDON PLACE

BRUCE ST

TWIST STREET

BANNET STREET

CLAIM STREET

ABEL ROAD

HARLEY STREET

Old
Fort

HILLBROW

PRETORIA STREET

HIGHLANDS

KOTZE

STREET

Hillbrow
Hospital

Mervyn
King
Ridge
Trail

Pullingerkop

CHARLTON
TERRACE

vic
entre

Adler Museum
of the History
of Medicine

Andre
Huguenot
Theatre

Windybrow
Theatre

SARATOGA AVENUE

DOORNFONTEIN

Witwatersrand
Technikon

BERTRAMS ROAD

MIT
OLMARANS STREET

Jo'burg
Central
Station

STREET

KING STREET

Joubert
Park

Johannesburg
Art Gallery

Doornfontein
Station

SIEMERT ROAD

SIVEWRIGHT AVENUE

NEW
DOORNFONTEIN

Alhambra
Theatre

Ellis
Park

South African
Transport Museum

CLAIM STREET

St Mary's
Cathedral

Union
Grounds

Ellis Park
Sports
Stadium

Ellis
Park
Station

Bruma
Fleamarket
World

BEZUIDENHOUT AVENUE

BREE STREET

JEPPE STREET

TWIST STREET

VON WIELLIGH STREET

PRITCHARD ST

Supreme
Court

MARKET STREET

CITY AND SUBURBAN

COMMISSIONER STREET

Jeppe Station

City
Hall

GPO

First National
Bank Museum

Jewish
Museum

Carlton Centre
and Panorama

Mynhardts

MARSHALL STREET

PARK STREET

Rand
Club

Standard
Bank
Gallery

PISEK ST

ELOFFE STREET

MARSHALLTOWN

ROSETTENVILLE ROAD

ANDERSON STREET

MOTORWAY
EXTENSION

ELOFF STREET

WEMMER

M2

James Hall
Transport Museum
& Wemmer Pan

HEDELBERG ROAD

✚ 68B4

Johannesburg Zoo
🖼 Jan Smuts Avenue,
   Parkview
☎ 011-646 2000
🕐 Daily 8:30–5:30
♿ Very good
💶 Moderate

JOHANNESBURG ZOO AND ZOO LAKE ✪

Even if you don't like the idea of animals in enclosures, this zoo is well worth visiting for its lovely grounds. Indigenous animals such as lions, elephants and penguins can be seen, as well as exotic tapirs, kangaroos and polar bears.

Zoo Lake, across the road, is a favourite with locals wanting a day out, with spacious lawns for picnicking, a restaurant, and rowing boats for hire. Open-air art exhibitions are held here monthly.

✚ 68B2
✉ 121 Bree Street
☎ 011-833 5624; fax
   011-833 5636;
   e-mail:
   museumafrica@
   joburg.org.za
🕐 Tue–Sun 9–5
🍴 Café (£)
♿ Good
💶 Cheap
↔ Newtown
   Cultural Precinct
   (▶ below)

MUSEUMAFRICA ✪✪✪

If you visit only one museum while in South Africa, it should be this beautifully designed space. A number of smaller museums formerly dispersed through Johannesburg are housed together here under one roof. The Geological Museum has a wonderful display of rocks and crystals, while the Bensusan Museum of Photography fully illustrates the art of the camera from its beginnings to the present. The section called 'Johannesburg Transformations' is devoted to the history of the city and its inhabitants. Elsewhere you can see outstanding examples of Bushman rock paintings and traditional African arts, with a wealth of information on the exhibits.

✚ 68B2
✉ Between Diagonal Street
   and Oriental Plaza

Market Theatre
✉ Corner of Bree and
   Wolhuter streets, New
   Town
☎ 011-832 1641; e-mail
   admin@markettheatre.co.
   za

NEWTOWN CULTURAL PRECINCT ✪

At the heart of this grouping of cultural facilities is the **Market Theatre**, which became famous under apartheid for its oppositional protest theatre. The theatre gets its name from the old fresh produce market in which it is built – make sure you take a look at the fine 1911 *beaux arts* façade. The surrounding Precinct now comprises several performance spaces, museums, music venues, an art gallery and a variety of places to eat and drink.

Above: *African sculpture*
Right: *one of the colourful converted warehouses of the Newtown Cultural Precinct*

Riding the Big Wheel at the Randburg waterfront

PARKTOWN ✪

Developed on a hillside away from the city centre, this was Johannesburg's first garden suburb. Many gracious stone mansions were built here, several designed by Sir Herbert Baker, South Africa's best-known architect. Over recent decades office development has encroached alarmingly, but a number of the original houses remain. Baker's own home, Stone Cottage, survives, as does Moot Cottage, where Lord Alfred Milner met with his group of young imperial administrators, the so-called Kindergarten, around 1900.

🔲 68B4

ℹ️ Westcliff and Parktown
Heritage Trust
✉️ 21 Rockridge Road
☎️ 011-482 3349 (also fax);
www.home.intekom.com/parktown

RANDBURG WATERFRONT ✪

Cape Town started the trend and Johannesburg has followed with its very own – also extremely popular – waterfront development. This one is built around the shores of an artificial lake, fed by the Jukskei River. Shoppers have the choice of a large number of retail outlets, as well as the Harbour Flea Market with some 360 stalls. More than 50 restaurants and pubs offer a great variety of options for eating and drinking. In addition there are ten cinemas, fountains, watersports, a climbing wall, bungee jumping, a range where you can chip golf balls on to a floating island green, and a large entertainment complex for children.

🔲 68A4

✉️ Republic Road, Ferndale, Randburg, north Johannesburg

☎️ 011-789 5052; fax: 011-789 5033; e-mail: info@rwaterfront.co.za

🕐 Daily, 10 till late

♿ Variable, phone for details

SOUTH AFRICAN NATIONAL MUSEUM OF ✪
MILITARY HISTORY

Set on the edge of the fine gardens containing the Johannesburg Zoo (➤ 70), this highly rated museum is dedicated to the history of South Africa at war. Objects from World Wars I and II include displays of aircraft, artillery and tanks. A notable exhibit is a German one-man submarine. There are also collections of swords, guns, medals, flags, uniforms and documents relating to war.

🔲 68B4

✉️ 22 Erlswold Way, Saxonwold

☎️ 011-646 5513

🕐 Daily 9–4:30

♿ Good

💷 Cheap

↔️ Johannesburg Zoo (➤ 70)

The Magaliesberg

Distance
From Johannesburg 250km;
from Pretoria 200km

Time
From Johannesburg, 4 hours
without stops, 6 hours with
stops; from Pretoria, 3.5 hours
without stops, 5.5 hours with
stops

Start/end point
North Johannesburg,
Randburg/Sandton area; or
central Pretoria
✛ 54A3

Lunch or tea
Mount Grace Hotel (££)
✉ 2.4km from Magaliesburg
☎ 014-577 1350
❷ Booking advisable

This drive takes you out of the urban sprawl of Gauteng to
the low mountain range of the Magaliesberg.

*Take the R511 north from Johannesburg,
between Randburg and Sandton. After about
30km turn on to the N4 and head northwest in
the direction of Rustenburg. You will soon reach
the Magaliesberg at Hartebeespoort Dam.
(From Pretoria you can reach the same point by
taking the N4 west.)*

Hartebeespoort Dam is a popular local resort, offering
fishing, watersports, birdwatching and restaurants. (If you
wish to go down to the water take the turn-off to Kosmos.)

Continue west on the N4 to Rustenburg.

All along this stretch you will see the Magaliesberg Nature
Reserve, with the low ridge of the mountains on your left.

*Just before Rustenburg turn left on to the
R24/R30 and head south. After passing
over the mountain at Olifantsnek, turn
left on to the R24 to Maanhaarrand.*

Maanhaarrand ('ridge with a mane') is famous
for its many prehistoric rock engravings.

*Continue southeast from Maanhaarrand
on the R24 for just over 8km, then turn
left on to the R560 in the direction of
Hekpoort.*

*Brightly painted Ndebele
homestead*

Just to the north of Hekpoort the Boers defeated a large
British contingent at the Battle of Nooitgedacht in
December 1900, during the Anglo-Boer War.

*From Hekpoort continue northeast along the
R560 for 21.5km, then turn right on to the
R512, and right again on to the R28, which
returns to Johannesburg. (If returning to
Pretoria, stay on the R512, which will take you
to the N4 back to Pretoria.)*

What to See Around Johannesburg

SOWETO ⭐⭐

Despite its African sounding name, Soweto is actually an acronym for 'South Western Townships'. Like all the other so-called 'townships' of South Africa, it was the product of the policies of racial segregation of successive white governments. The township began life in 1944 as a residential area for blacks, located some 20km southwest of the white suburbs of Johannesburg. Soweto expanded enormously in the 1950s, when many thousands of box-like, tin-roofed houses were built. The famous Soweto Uprising of 1976, started by schoolchildren protesting against Afrikaans as a compulsory subject, spelled the beginning of the end for white rule in South Africa. Today Soweto is a teeming, vibrant, often dangerous place: a mixture of shacklands, vast expanses of tiny houses and up-market residential areas. Tourists should visit only with people who know the area, or as part of an organised tour.

✚ 54A3

Jimmy's Face to Face Tours
✚ 130 Main Street, City Centre
☎ 011-331 6109; fax: 011-331 5388; e-mail: face2face@pixie.co.za
♿ Good
🍽 Moderate
❓ Variety of tours offered, with or without meal; also night tours

Soweto roofscape

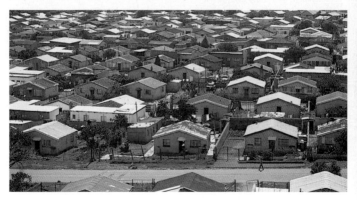

STERKFONTEIN CAVES ⭐⭐

Situated some 20km northwest of Johannesburg, these caves were declared a World Heritage Site in 1999 in recognition of their unique importance for the study of human origins. Starting with the discovery of the first adult skull of *Australopithecus africanus* (Southern African ape-man) in the caves in 1936, spectacular finds of early human-like fossils have continued right up to the present. Very recently, in separate discoveries, the most complete skeleton and skull yet of early hominids have been found. At the site you can view the caves, a large underground lake and the Robert Broom Museum of fossils.

✚ 54A3
✉ Off the R563, about 8km northwest of Krugersdorp
☎ 011-956 6342 (also fax)
🕐 Tue–Sun 9–4 (tours every 30 mins, lasting 1 hour)
🍽 Café (£)
♿ None
🗝 Moderate

Pretoria

 54A3
ℹ️ Tourist Office ☎ 012-310 3911

Glowing jacarandas in a Pretoria street

The quiet city of Pretoria, with its jacaranda-lined streets, was formerly the capital of the old Boer republic of the Transvaal. It was occupied by British forces in June 1900, during the Anglo-Boer War. When the different parts of South Africa came together to form the Union in 1910, Pretoria became the administrative capital, a role it retains in the 'New' South Africa.

What to See in Pretoria

 54A3
✉️ 149 Visagie Street
☎ 012-324 6082; fax: 012-328 5173; e-mail: awindow1@nchm.co.za
🕐 Daily 8–4
🍴 Restaurant (££)
♿ Good
💵 Cheap

AFRICAN WINDOW ✪✪
This innovative complex brings together items selected from many Pretoria museums to give an overview of the different cultures of South Africa. Clothing, toys, jewellery, artefacts and objects of archaeological and anthropological interest are on display. A special exhibit highlights the lifestyle of the Hananwa people of the Blue Mountains, and there are fine examples of Bushman rock art, as well as live demonstrations of traditional cooking, music and dance.

 54A3
✉️ 275 Jacob Mare Street
☎ 012-322 2805; fax: 012-320 2742; e-mail: melrosehouse@intekom.co.za
🕐 Tue–Sun 10–5
♿ None
💵 Cheap

MELROSE HOUSE ✪
This strange house, with its two odd gables, deep veranda and elaborate ironwork, was built by George Heys, a successful stage-coach operator in 1886. Its wallpapered rooms, paintings and heavy furniture give a vivid idea of the way of life of a wealthy businessman in the Transvaal of the 19th century. A stained-glass window depicts Sir Walter Scott's *Lay of the Last Minstrel*. The Treaty of Vereeniging that ended the Anglo-Boer War was signed in the dining room on 31 May 1902.

NATIONAL ZOOLOGICAL GARDENS ✪✪✪

Generally rated the best in South Africa, Pretoria's zoo is set in beautiful gardens, with an ornate Victorian fountain. A highlight is the zoo's cableway, giving passengers a bird's-eye view of the gardens. On the ground you can see several thousand animals, comprising around 120 species, housed in good re-creations of natural settings. Among them are most of South Africa's major species, including rarities such as the brown hyena and pigmy hippo, as well as bears, tapirs and apes from elsewhere in the world.

🚩 54A3
✉ 232 Boom Street
☎ 012-328 3265; fax: 012-323 4540
🕐 Daily 8–5:30
🍴 Restaurant (££), kiosk (£)
♿ Good 👍 Cheap

The eccentric façade of Melrose House

PAUL KRUGER HOUSE MUSEUM ✪

Paul Kruger, most famous of all Afrikaners, was President of the Transvaal Republic from 1883 to 1900. The plain, twin-gabled house in which he lived throughout that period is now a museum. On view here are his desk, a collection of his pipes, a flag of the old Republic and one of the first telephones to be installed in Pretoria. A particularly gruesome exhibit is the knife Kruger used to amputate his thumb after a hunting accident. Out the back are his private rail coach and state coach.

🚩 54A3
✉ 60 Church Street
☎ 012-326 9172
🕐 Mon–Fri 8:30–4:30, Sat–Sun 9–4:30
♿ Good 👍 Cheap

Sculpted portrait of Paul Kruger

TRANSVAAL MUSEUM ✪

For bird-lovers this museum, focusing mainly on natural history, is not to be missed. In the Austin Roberts Bird Hall, named after the author of the standard guide to the birds of the region, you will find a comprehensive display of stuffed birds of Southern Africa, and can listen to the recorded call of each bird. Elsewhere in the museum are a dodo skeleton and mammal and reptile galleries.

🚩 54A3
✉ 432 Paul Kruger Street
☎ 012-322 7632; e-mail: kemp@nfi.co.za
🕐 Mon–Sat 9–5, Sun and public holidays 11–5
🍴 Restaurant (££)
♿ Good 👍 Cheap

75

UNION BUILDINGS ✪

- 54A3
- Government Avenue
- 012-310 3911
- No access to inside of buildings; ask police on duty for permission to view outside
- None

The imposing exterior of Sir Herbert Baker's Union Buildings in Pretoria

The Union Buildings are the masterpiece of architect Sir Herbert Baker. The majestic structure, with its two wings, each with its own tower, and linked by a graceful colonnaded amphitheatre, was built to mark the formation of the Union of South Africa in 1910. It has been the seat of the executive of successive governments, most recently that of the post-1994 ANC government. The amphitheatre has witnessed many historic events – a funeral service was held here in 1966 for Hendrik Verwoerd, the architect of apartheid, and the country's most recent presidents, Nelson Mandela and Thabo Mbeki, were sworn in here.

VOORTREKKER MONUMENT AND MUSEUM ✪✪

- 54A3
- Monument Hill, 6km from city centre
- 012-321 6990 (also fax)
- Daily 8–5; Wed 8–8. Closed Good Friday, 25 Dec
- Restaurant (££), kiosk (£)
- Good
- Moderate
- Phone for guided tours

Sculpture of Voortrekker leader Piet Retief at the Voortrekker Monument

This monument to the outdated ideology of Afrikaner nationalism remains strangely moving. The massive granite edifice, 40m high and set on a base 40m square, was opened in December 1949. The outside of the building bristles with symbols: a wall of ox-wagons, a barrier of Zulu spears, reliefs of wild animals, busts of Voortrekker leaders, a statue of a Voortrekker woman and children. The most striking feature of the interior is the

monumental marble frieze, 92m long, showing the Great Trek, in which Afrikaner pioneers journeyed to the interior of South Africa. Although its generally demeaning portrayal of blacks is offensive, the frieze is a powerful piece of work. In the nearby museum, tapestries depicting the Great Trek, and Voortrekker possessions and weapons are on display.

Pretoria Centre

This walk takes you through the historic centre of the city.

Start from Church Square.

A bronze statue of Paul Kruger is appropriately the focal point of this square, the heart of old Pretoria. Take a look at the impressive façades of the buildings around the square: the Old Raadsaal (council chamber) where Kruger's government met; Sir Herbert Baker's Reserve Bank building; and the old Palace of Justice.

Walk west along Church Street for five blocks to Heroes' Acre, and then return to Church Square.

Halfway along you pass the Paul Kruger House Museum (► 75). In Heroes' Acre are the graves of Andries Pretorius (after whom Pretoria is named), Paul Kruger and Hendrik Verwoerd, and also, oddly, that of the Australian 'Breaker' Morant, executed by the British in 1902 for allegedly murdering a Boer prisoner and a missionary.

From Church Square walk east. You will come first to J G Strijdom Square, then to the State Theatre and Opera House. Opposite the theatre is Sammy Marks Square.

Sammy Marks Square commemorates the eccentric, illiterate Randlord of the same name.

Turn right from Church Street into Prinsloo Street. Walk south for six blocks, then turn right into Jacob Mare Street and continue two blocks to Paul Kruger Street.

After passing Melrose House (► 74) on your left, look left down Paul Kruger Street and you will see the Italian renaissance-style façade of Sir Herbert Baker's railway station.

With the railway station behind you, walk north up Paul Kruger Street back to Church Square.

Distance
4km

Time
1.5 hours without stops;
4 hours with stops

Start/end point
Church Square
➕ 54A3

Lunch or tea
Café Riche (£–££)
✉ 2 Church Square
(southwest corner)
☎ 012-328 3173

Food & Drink

South Africa's indigenous and immigrant population, and its diversity of climates, have created the country's varied culinary traditions. Imported recipes, adapted over the centuries with the inclusion of local ingredients and innovative cooking methods have given it its originality.

African Cuisine

Traditional staples are meat (*nyama*), usually roasted or boiled, a white porridge (*pap*) made from maize, and wild spinach (Zulu *imifino*, Sotho *morogo*). Nowadays the *pap* is often eaten with a spicy stew of meat, onions, tomatoes and peppers. Mopani worms, dried caterpillars of the emperor moth, are an acquired taste.

Immigrant Cuisine

Most of the international types of food – Indian, Chinese, French, Italian, British – can be found in the cities. The Portuguese in Southern Africa have developed their own distinctive style of chicken and seafood dishes spiced with peri-peri, a concoction of chillies and peppers.

Indonesian (Malay) & Afrikaner Cuisine

So-called 'Cape Malay' slaves, mainly from Indonesia, had a very strong influence on Dutch and then Afrikaner cooking, resulting in many of the foods now thought of as typically South African. Among these are delicious *bredies*, stews of vegetables and/or meat – best known are those made with tomatoes or *waterblommetjies*, a kind of water-lily. Other specialities are *bobotie*, made with curried mince and egg, *sosaties* (spicy kebabs), *konfyt* (a range of sweet fruit preserves), and *blatjang* (tasty fruit chutney). For sweets try *koeksisters*, twisted deep-fried doughnuts, dipped in syrup.

Salad, sosaties and boerewors are an essential part of the South African barbeque

Barbecues and Meats

The barbecue (*braai*) is a South African institution. Expect to eat quantities of grilled steak, chops, kebabs, chicken and, above all, *boerewors*, a sausage of coarse-ground spiced meat. Typical accompaniments are a green salad and beer.

Unusual meats can be found at some restaurants: game of various kinds, such as springbok, impala, kudu and warthog, as well as ostrich, now quite common, and guinea-fowl. A great local favourite is *biltong*, dried and seasoned meat – usually beef or game.

A delicious harvest from South African coastal waters

Seafood

In most coastal cities and towns you can find excellent fresh seafood. The West Coast specialises in lobsters and mussels. Try Cape salmon, firm-fleshed *kabeljou* (kob), *perlemoen* (abalone – if you're lucky enough to find it), octopus and calamari in the Western Cape. Knysna is renowned for its delicious fresh oysters, while the East Coast, especially Durban, is famous for its fine prawns and shrimps.

Fruit

The country's various climatic zones produce fresh fruit of all kinds: in the subtropical northeast, pawpaws, mangos and bananas; on the highveld, oranges, grapefruit and *naartjies* (tangerines); in the southwest, grapes and deciduous fruits such as apples, pears and apricots. For something unusual, try the peeled fruit of the prickly pear in the Eastern Cape.

Products of a centuries-old tradition of wine making

Drink

The best-known traditional African drinks are *tshwala*, a thick beer made from fermented sorghum and water, and *amasi*, a yoghurt-like drink of thick curdled milk.

The Western Cape, with its Mediterranean climate, has been making wine for more than 300 years, and now exports it all over the world. Because of the relatively hot summers, the reds are strong and full-bodied, the most popular types being cabernet sauvignon, shiraz and the local pinotage. The white wines – riesling, sauvignon blanc and chardonnay – have a crisp, slightly fruity flavour. Good fortified wines and brandy are also made locally.

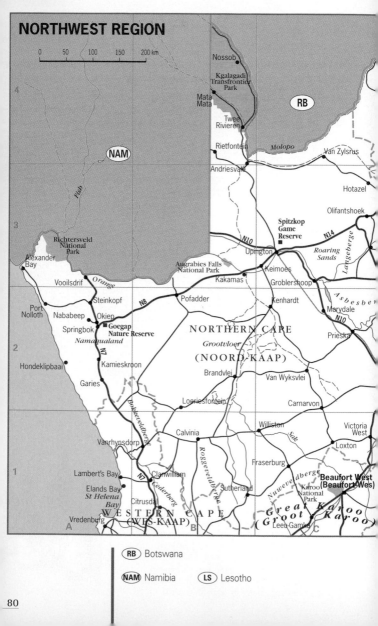

NORTHWEST REGION

0   50   100   150   200 km

Nossob

Kgalagadi Transfrontier Park

Mata Mata

RB

Twee Rivieren

Molopo

Van Zylsrus

Rietfontein

NAM

Andriesvale

Hotazel

Fish

Olifantshoek

Spitzkop Game Reserve

N10

Upington

Roaring Sands

N14

Langeberge

Richtersveld National Park

Augrabies Falls National Park

Keimoes

Alexander Bay

Vooilsdrif

Orange

Kakamas

Groblershoop

Asbesber

Port Nolloth

Steinkopf

N8

Pofadder

Kenhardt

Marydale

Nababeep   Okiep

N10

Springbok   Goegap Nature Reserve

NORTHERN CAPE

Prieska

Namaqualand

N7

(NOORD-KAAP)

Grootvloer

Hondeklipbaai

Kamieskroon

Brandvlei

Van Wyksvlei

Garies

Carnarvon

Loeriesfontein

Brakrivierberge

Williston

Victoria West

Calvinia

Sak

Loxton

Vanrhynsdorp

Roggeveldberge

Fraserburg

Nuweveldberge

Beaufort West (Beaufort-Wes)

Lambert's Bay

N7

Clanwilliam

Sutherland

Karoo National Park

Elands Bay   St Helena Bay

Kederberg

Citrusdal

Great Karoo (Groot Karoo)

Vredenburg

WESTERN CAPE (WES-KAAP)

Leeu-Gamka

RB Botswana

NAM Namibia   **LS** Lesotho

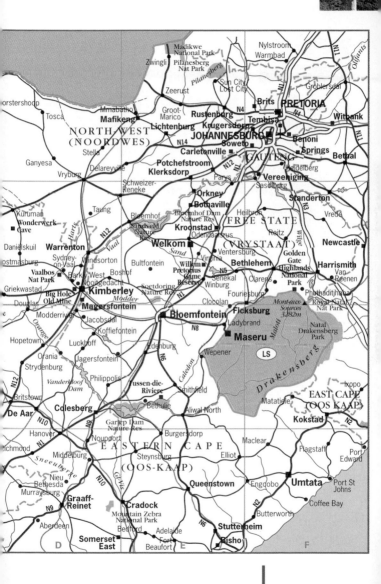

Northwest Region

This vast thinly populated area, mountainous in the east, comprises rolling prairie, maize fields, Karoo scrub and semi-desert. Small numbers of Bushmen still live here, descendants of the bands of hunter-gatherers who used to roam these arid expanses.

The economy of the region relies on agriculture, sustained in many places by irrigation from the Vaal and Orange rivers, and on the mining of diamonds around Kimberley and gold in the Free State. With the growth of tourism in South Africa, many farmers have turned to game farming to attract commercial hunters to the area.

Visitors come to the region for the fine game reserves, the spring flowers of the Northern Cape, and for peace and quiet. The more active will find rafting and canoeing on the Orange River, many recently opened 4x4 trails, and a variety of hiking trails through rugged, sun-scorched landscapes.

'There is a contentment and general prosperity about Bloemfontein which is apt to make a dweller in busy cities think that though it might not quite suit himself, it would be very good for everybody else.'

ANTHONY TROLLOPE,
South Africa (1878)

Kimberley

The history of Kimberley, capital of the Northern Cape, is inseparable from the colourful story of diamond mining in South Africa. The fabulous treasure-house of diamonds, the Big Hole (▶ 21), was the centre from which the city of Kimberley grew. The present population is about 200,000.

Named after the British Colonial Secretary of the time, the Earl of Kimberley, the city was founded in 1871. In 1878, when it was first granted municipal status, Kimberley was still a rough miners' camp of tin shanties and tents, but from then on things improved rapidly. In 1882 this was the first African city to get electric street lights, and in 1887 trams started to run.

Two men dominated early Kimberley and the diamond business. One was Barney Barnato, a former barman, boxer and music-hall artiste from the East End of London who came to South Africa in 1873. Starting out as a digger and diamond-buyer, he became a multimillionaire by the age of 25. Barnato's great rival was Cecil John Rhodes. The son of an English clergyman, Rhodes came to South Africa in 1870, at the age of 17, and quickly amassed a fortune. When Rhodes's company De Beers Consolidated Mines bought out Barnato in 1888, De Beers gained a monopoly over the trade in diamonds only recently relinquished.

During the Anglo-Boer War, the Boers besieged Kimberley for four months. Famous battles were fought near the city at Modderrivier and Magersfontein, where trenches were used for the first time in modern warfare when the Boers dug in below the hill at Magersfontein.

The diamond mines at Kimberley still produce some 4,000 carats of diamonds a day.

> **DID YOU KNOW?**
> Kimberley once had the world's only drive-in pubs, the West End Hotel and the Halfway Hotel.

Colonial elegance, the Kimberley City Hall and, inset, a memento of Barney Barnato in the Kimberley Mine Museum

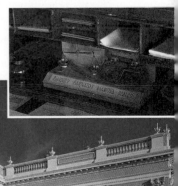

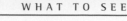

81D3

Tucker Street

053-839 4930/1/2

Daily, summer 8–6, winter 8–5:30. Closed Good Friday, 25 Dec

Restaurant (£)

Being upgraded; phone in advance

Moderate

Below: *reconstructed pub in the Kimberley Mine Museum*

81D3

Molyneaux Road

053-842 1321

Surface tours Mon–Fri 9, 11

Tours: surface: cheap; underground: expensive

81D3

Atlas and Chapel streets

053-839 2700

Mon–Fri 9–5, Sat 9–5, Sun 2–5

Good

Cheap

What to See in Kimberley

THE BIG HOLE AND KIMBERLEY MINE MUSEUM ✪✪✪

A tram route runs to the Big Hole from the centre of Kimberley. The Big Hole (► 21) and, on its rim, the streets and buildings of the open-air Kimberley Mine Museum, give visitors a strong sense of old Kimberley. Original offices, private houses, a church, a pub, a pawnbroker's shop, a blacksmith's workshop and Barney Barnato's Boxing Academy can be visited, and photographs portray city life during the diamond rush. In the diamond exhibition hall 2,000 carats of real diamonds are on display, alongside replicas of some of the world's most famous gems. Near by, the 19th-century pub, the Star of the West (► 58), offers refreshment.

BULTFONTEIN MINE TOURS ✪

Bultfontein was the place where diamonds were first discovered in 1869. The De Beers company now operates the diamond mine here and offers tours of the surface workings (minimum age seven years) which take you through the treatment and recovery plant; underground tours (minimum age 16 years) are by appointment only.

MCGREGOR MUSEUM ✪

Named after a former mayor of the city, this museum is housed in what was the old Sanatorium where Rhodes lived during the Siege of Kimberley in 1899. It focuses on the plants and animals of the area, and on the history of Kimberley. A satellite institution, the Alexander Mcgregor Memorial Museum, concentrates on geology, but also has displays on the history of the Northern Cape.

Above: *a blue wildebeest and its calf grazing side by side*
Left: *the spectacular Augrabies Falls*

What to See in the Northern Cape

AUGRABIES FALLS NATIONAL PARK ⚫⚫

At the heart of this 28,000ha park lie the Augrabies Falls – the name means 'place of the great noise' in the Khoikhoi language. At its peak, in summer, over 400 million litres of water a minute plunge 65m down the granite cascade into an abyss of unknown depth, where a legendary 'water monkey' is said to lurk. Over millennia, the torrent has scoured out a deep, narrow ravine 18km long below the Falls. The park offers game drives and a three-day hiking trail through a rocky, moonlike landscape, set with beautiful, branching quiver trees.

✚ 80B3
✉ 120km west of Upington
☎ 012-428 9111; e-mail: reservations@parks-sa.co.za
🕐 Daily 6:30AM–10PM (reception open 7–7)
🍴 Restaurant (££)
♿ Good
🍺 Cheap

COLESBERG ⚫

This pretty town in the heart of the Karoo is a great place to get away from it all. Motorists often stay overnight here to break their journey between Gauteng and the Western Cape. Founded in 1830, Colesberg still has many of its 19th-century private houses, churches and public buildings. There are several pleasant bed-and-breakfasts and restaurants in the town, as well as an atmospheric pub in the old mill house.

✚ 81D2
ℹ Tourist Information
✉ Museum Square, Murray Street ☎ 051-753 0678; e-mail: belinda@mjvn.co.za

KGALAGADI TRANSFRONTIER PARK ⚫⚫

The former Kalahari Gemsbok Park in South Africa and its sister park in Botswana have recently fused to create a unique cross-border reserve of 38,000sq km, nearly twice the size of Israel. This vast size allows for a phenomenon once common in Africa: the large-scale nomadic and seasonal movement of animals.

Despite its dryness, the park is home to the Big Five (► 6) and the magnificent gemsbok with its black and white masked face, as well as springbok, eland, wildebeest, brown hyena, cheetah and many birds, including large numbers of raptors (birds of prey).

✚ 80B4
✉ 360km north of Upington
☎ 054-561 2000; fax: 054-561 2005 (Park); 012-346 6065 (bookings – 24 hours)
🕐 Daily 7:30–6:30
🍴 Restaurant (££)
♿ None
🍺 Moderate

Rock, hills and dry scrub making up a typical Namaqualand scene

 80A2
Springbok Tourist Office
☎ 027-712 8035; fax:
027-712 1421; e-mail:
tourismsbk@namakwa/
dm.co.za

NAMAQUALAND ✪✪✪

This area of the Northern Cape, south of the Orange River, is at its best in spring, when it is transformed into a carpet of brilliantly coloured flowers (▶ 24). A good place to see the spring flowers, as well as 94 species of bird and 45 species of mammal, is the Goegap Nature Reserve, 15km east of Springbok. This, the region's main town, is increasingly becoming a centre for outdoor adventure activities – camping, hiking and 4x4 trailing.

In the extreme northwest corner of Namaqualand lies the mountainous, starkly beautiful Richtersveld National Park. An astonishing variety of small mammals, reptiles, birds and plant life manages to survive in the harsh, dry climate. Here you can see the weird succulent tree, the '*halfmens*' (half man, from its appearance), *Pachypodium namaquanum*.

 80C3
Tourist Office ☎ 054-332
6064 (also fax); e-mail:
tourism@kharahaismunici
pality.co.za ⏰ Mon–Fri
8–5:30, Sat 9–12

Spitskop Game Reserve
⊠ 13km northwest of
Upington
☎ 054-332 1336

UPINGTON ✪

Police mounted on camels used to operate out of Upington, the main town on the Orange River. Unlikely as it may seem in this semi-desert region, the town is now a centre for grape growing due to extensive irrigation from the river. The grapes are used mainly for raisins and sultanas, but wine is also produced here.

A number of companies use Upington as a base for canoeing and river-rafting safaris on the Orange. Worth a visit are Olyvenhout Island, with its 1,000m avenue of date palms, and the nearby 5,641ha **Spitskop Game Reserve**.

What to See in the Northwest Province

PILANESBERG NATIONAL PARK ⬤⬤

Lake Mankwe, in the crater of an extinct volcano, lies at the centre of this 55,000ha park. A number of local farmers were displaced to create the reserve in the 1970s and a massive programme of relocation of animals was undertaken. The Big Five (➤ 6) are now to be seen here, as are more than 300 species of bird, many types of antelope, eland, giraffe, zebra and hippo. Because the park lies in a transitional ecological zone, springbok and impala can, very unusually, be seen together here. The low-set hides near waterholes make for excellent game viewing. Hot-air balloon trips over the reserve are available. This park is situated close to both Johannesburg and Pretoria, making it ideal for a short weekend break.

SUN CITY ⬤⬤

Some two hours' drive northwest of Johannesburg lies the entertainment and holiday resort of Sun City. Connoisseurs of kitsch will love this place, which actually consists of two parts: the newer Lost City, and the older Sun City.

The Lost City follows a theme, attempting to re-create *King Solomon's Mines*, a novel by the colonial writer H Rider Haggard. At the two 'Cities' you will find an artificial beach, complete with artificial surf, a casino, American-style showgirl-extravaganzas, golf courses with real crocodiles in the water hazard, playgrounds and a petting zoo for the children. If you need to get back to nature, the Pilanesberg National Park (➤ above) is right next door.

+ 54A3
✉ 190km northwest of Johannesburg
☎ 014-555 5351/7; e-mail: tidcpberg@mweb.co.za (Park); 012-346 6065 (bookings)
🕐 Daily 6:30–6
🍴 Snack bar (£)
♿ None 👟 Moderate
↔ Sun City (➤ below)

Below: *inland surf at Sun City's Valley of the Waves and, inset, volcano bridge at the Lost City*

+ 54A3
✉ 190km northwest of Johannesburg
☎ 011-786 7000; fax: 011-780 7726; www.suninternational.com
🕐 Daily 8:30–5
🍴 Many outlets (£–£££)
♿ Very good

81E2

i Tourist Office ⊠ 60 Park Road, Willows ☎ 051-405 8490; fax: 051-447 3859; e-mail: blminfo@iafrica.com

National Museum
⊠ 36 Aliwal Street
☎ 051-447 9609
🕐 Mon–Sat 8–5, Sun 1–5:30
🍴 Restaurant (££)
♿ Few
✋ Cheap

Right: *the First Raadsaal, Bloemfontein, earliest meeting place of the old Orange Free State government*

🕇 81E2
⊠ 160km south of Bloemfontein
☎ 051-754 0071; fax: 051-754 0103; e-mail: gariepdam@internext.co.za

Above: *obelisk at the National Women's War Memorial*

What to See in the Free State

BLOEMFONTEIN

Bloemfontein ('flower fountain') was originally the capital of the old Boer Republic of the Orange Free State. At the formation of the Union in 1910 the city became and remains to this day the seat of the Appeal Court and judicial capital of South Africa. This is a worthy and pleasant, if slightly dull place. Maps are available for walking tours of the historic city centre around President Brand Street. Among the buildings included in the Conservation Area are the simple, thatched First Raadsaal (council chamber) with mud and dung floor, the more elaborate Fourth Raadsaal, and the Presidency, official residence of the head of the old republic. Within walking distance are the Appeal Court and the Queen's Fort of 1848. Highlights of the **National Museum** are the fossil collection and the re-creation of a 19th-century street. Naval Hill, a small nature reserve right in the centre of Bloemfontein, provides good views over the city.

Not to be missed is the National Women's Memorial and War Museum, showing the horror of the concentration camps in which the British imprisoned civilians during the Anglo-Boer War. More than 40,000 Africans and Afrikaners died in these camps.

GARIEP DAM ✪

When full, this dam on the Orange and Caledon rivers creates a lake that covers 374sq km, South Africa's largest inland body of water. The dam wall is 914m long and extensive tunnels from here feed irrigation systems up to 80km away. Bordering the dam is the 11,200ha Gariep Nature Reserve, with its considerable herds of game.

GOLDEN GATE HIGHLANDS NATIONAL PARK (▶ 20, TOP TEN)

Along the Eastern Highlands of the Free State

This drive takes you through superb countryside alongside South Africa's border with Lesotho.

Take the R712 from Golden Gate Highlands National Park (➤ 20) to the town of Clarens, 18km away.

Clarens, named after the Swiss resort where President Paul Kruger died in 1904, is beautifully situated below golden sandstone cliffs. Many artists have come to live here, and the town has restaurants, gift shops and a very good bookshop.

From Clarens drive southwest on the R711. After 36km you will reach Fouriesburg.

The road passes by picturesque sandstone outcrops, forming low flat-topped hills. All along this stretch to your left are Lesotho's Maluti Mountains, often capped with snow in winter. Look out for signs directing you to the many Bushman rock paintings in the area. Fouriesburg, founded in 1892, was the seat of the Orange Free State government for a time during the Anglo-Boer War. Excellent meals can be had at the Fouriesburg Country Inn.

Maluti Mountains, Lesotho

Just after Fouriesburg is a T-junction. Turn left here on to the R26 in the direction of Ficksburg, 56km away.

The town of Ficksburg, situated 5km from a major entry point into Lesotho, is very much a border town, with hundreds of people coming in every day from Lesotho to shop. A Cherry Festival and a Vintage Tractor Show are held here annually (➤ 116).

From Ficksburg, if you have the time, you can continue southwest on the R26 to the town of Clocolan. Return to Golden Gate along the same route.

Distance
220km (290km if you go on to Clocolan)

Time
3 hours without stops; 6 hours with stops

Start/end point
Golden Gate Highlands National Park
➕ 81F3

Tea or Lunch
Fouriesburg Country Inn (£–££)
✉ Reitz Street
☎ 058-223 0207

89

Lesotho

81F2
Tourist Office
Maseru 092662-291 0276

The mountain kingdom of Lesotho, entirely surrounded by South Africa, owes its existence to the statesman Moshoeshoe (pronounced Moshwehshweh). Through much of the 19th century he managed to protect the Basotho people he had gathered together on the impregnable flat-topped hill, Thaba Bosiu ('mountain of the night'), against many enemies – other tribes, Boers, Britons. In 1884 the country came under British rule, and in 1966 it attained independence as a constitutional monarchy.

Almost all of Lesotho is rugged and mountainous, with few good roads. The country's great attraction is its spectacular scenery, with many clear streams and rivers, sandstone caves (often with Bushman paintings), and mountain slopes dotted with traditional homesteads. Multi-day, or shorter hiking, pony trekking and 4x4 trails are available, as are excellent opportunities for trout fishing and birdwatching. The country is known for its rugs and goods woven from grass, wool and mohair. Look out for the distinctive Basotho grass hats – conical in shape with a large knob on top.

The Lesotho Highlands Water Scheme, a colossal engineering project of the late 20th century, has created the Katse Dam in the centre of Lesotho, which provides water to South Africa via an elaborate system of tunnels and canals. It can be reached by an excellent road, and the views are stunning.

Also worth visiting is the capital, Maseru, where you can buy arts and crafts. Thaba Bosiu, near by, is a sacred place for the people of Lesotho; the graves of Moshoeshoe and other leading national figures are here.

Pony trekking through the rugged mountains of Lesotho

Where To...

Above: scenic Swadini Dam in the Blyde River Canyon
Right: a common road sign in rural South Africa, 'Danger, antelope crossing'

Western & Eastern Cape

Prices
Prices give the approximate cost of a meal for one person, not including wine and tips:

£ = under 60 Rand
££ = 60–100 Rand
£££ = above 100 Rand

Dress Code
The dress code, such as it is, at most South African restaurants is described locally as smart-casual, meaning shirt and trousers (no bare torsos or bathing costumes). Very few establishments require men to wear a jacket and tie.

Wine
The cost of wine in restaurants can be anything from 30 to 80 per cent more than you would pay in a liquor store. Some restaurants will let you bring your own wine (BYO) without extra charge. Others charge R10–R20 corkage. Phone in advance and ask.

Western Cape

Cape Town

Africa Café (£–££)
Provides an authentic African eating experience, serving a variety of beef, chicken and lamb dishes from across the continent. For vegetarians there are Kenyan vegetable pâtés or Moroccan couscous salad.
✉ 108 Shortmarket Street ☎ 021-422 0221 🕐 Dinner Mon–Sat

Aubergine (££–£££)
Classic cuisine served al fresco in a shady courtyard. South African specialities feature on the menu here, as well as dishes such as quails and aubergine soufflé.
✉ 39 Barnet Street, Gardens ☎ 021-465 4909 🕐 Lunch Thu only; dinner Mon–Sat

Au Jardin (££–£££)
You can look forward to fine dining with fabulous mountain views at this French-style restaurant. The menu changes daily and fresh, seasonal ingredients are used.
✉ Vineyard Hotel, Colinton Road, Newlands ☎ 021-683 1520 🕐 Lunch Tue–Fri; dinner Mon–Sat

Café Bardeli (£–££)
Very cool café and bar hang-out for TV and media people, serving tapas, snacks, good salads and cakes.
✉ Longkloof Studios, off Kloof Street ☎ 021-423 4444 🕐 Breakfast, teas, lunch, dinner daily

Cape Colony Restaurant (£££)
Beautifully proportioned interior with a mural of old Cape Town and a domed ceiling. The food is exceptionally good – there is something to please most palates – but with a strong South African accent. One of Cape Town's best restaurants.
✉ Mount Nelson Hotel, 76 Orange Street ☎ 021-483 1000 🕐 Lunch, dinner daily

Constantia Uitsig (££–£££)
Set in beautiful vineyards, this restaurant is consistently rated one of Cape Town's best. The menu features excellent red meat, seafood and pasta dishes.
✉ Uitsig Farm, Constantia ☎ 021-794 4480 🕐 Lunch, dinner Tue–Sun

Emily's (££–£££)
The décor inside is colourful, the delicious food is an outstanding blend of local and international styles, and the wine list is comprehensive.
✉ Victoria and Alfred Waterfront ☎ 021-421 1133 🕐 Lunch, dinner Mon–Sat

Morituri (£)
If you're on a low budget and you're looking for pizza, this restaurant serves the best in town, on a thin base with a good range of delicious toppings.
✉ 214 Main Road, Claremont ☎ 021-683 6671 🕐 Lunch Mon–Fri; dinner daily

Ocean Basket (£–££)
This is a good seafood restaurant offering South African specialities and a sushi bar.
✉ Victoria and Alfred Waterfront ☎ 021-419 4300 🕐 Lunch, dinner daily

Savoy Cabbage (££–£££)
Fresh food simply cooked is the motto of this outstanding restaurant. Despite the name, not everything comes with cabbage; they also serve fine seafood, interesting tripe and liver dishes, and delicious desserts.

✉ 101 Hout Street ☎ 021-424 2626 ⏰ Lunch Mon–Fri; dinner Mon–Sat

Darling
Evita se Perron (£–££)
This unique cabaret-restaurant, situated in an old railway building serves traditional South African specialities such as *bredies* and *bobotie*.

✉ Old Darling Railway Station ☎ 022-492 2831 ⏰ Breakfast, lunch and dinner daily

Franschhoek
Monneaux (£££)
Monneaux is one of the country's top restaurants; the emphasis here is on modern French cuisine and local wines.

✉ Franschhoek Country House, Main Road ☎ 021-876-3386 ⏰ Lunch daily; dinner Mon–Sat

Montagu
Four Oaks Restaurant (££)
An elegant restaurant housed in a mid-19th-century thatched cottage, now a national monument. Small, regularly changing menu, good on pastas and German dishes.

✉ 46 Long Street, Montagu ☎ 023-614 2778 ⏰ Lunch, dinner Tue–Sun

Paarl
Rhebokskloof Estate (££–£££)
Restaurant on a beautiful wine estate, with a menu ranging from soups and fresh salads to grilled fish and meat.

✉ Rhebokskloof Estate, North Paarl ☎ 021-869 8606 ⏰ Lunch Tue–Thu; dinner Thu–Mon

Stellenbosch
Decameron (££–£££)
The Decameron features Italian and general cuisine complemented by a good selection of local Stellenbosch wines.

✉ 50 Plein Street ☎ 021-883 3331 ⏰ Lunch Mon–Sun; dinner Mon–Sat

Swellendam
Zanddrift (££)
Set in an 18th-century cottage, this restaurant in the Drostdy Museum (➤ 44) offers excellent country-fresh fare: soups, pâtés, deep-fried mushrooms and cheesecake.

✉ Swellengrebel Street ☎ 028-514 1789 ⏰ Breakfast, tea and lunch daily (phone in advance)

Tulbagh
Paddagang Wine House (£–££)
Cape farmhouse fare served either in an old thatched wine house or under a shady pergola; very good wine list.

✉ 23 Church Street ☎ 023-230 0394 ⏰ Breakfast, teas, lunch daily

Garden Route

George
The King Fisher (££)
Good seafood menu offering fresh fish daily, excellent prawns, and calamari and kingklip specialities. The

Liquor Stores
The sale of liquor in South Africa is still somewhat restricted. Until very recently it was difficult for restaurants to get a liquor licence, but now most have one. Outside of licensed premises, liquor is sold at specialized 'bottlestores', open daily except Sunday. Because of a quirk in the law, supermarkets can sell wine (except on Sundays) but not beer.

Tipping
Very few eateries include a service charge in the bill. The norm is to tip around 10–15 per cent, depending on the quality of the service you have received. Be generous if you can afford it: there is no minimum wage in South Africa, so waiters and waitresses are often paid extremely poorly, and rely heavily on tips to boost their income.

Monkey Gland Sauce
Diners at steakhouses may be startled to see something called 'monkey gland sauce' on the menu. Rest assured that the sauce has nothing to do with monkeys or their glands. The name was jokingly given by its inventor to a piquant sauce of onion, tomato, fruit chutney and Worcestershire sauce designed to spice up steak and other cuts of meat.

menu also lists good pizzas and salads.
✉ 1 Courtenay Street ☎ 044-873 3127 🕐 Lunch, dinner daily

Knysna
The Pink Umbrella(£–££)
Al fresco dining in summer in the beautiful garden, or in the pleasant dining-room. Gourmet fish and meat dishes, with vegetarian meals a speciality.
✉ 14 Kingsway, Leisure Island ☎ 044-384 0135 🕐 Lunch, dinner daily; closed Mon

Plettenberg Bay
Moby Dick's Seafood Bistro (££)
Seafood is the speciality here, but local meats such as Karoo lamb and ostrich are also served. Whale-watching deck upstairs.
✉ Central Beach ☎ 044-533 3682 🕐 Breakfast, lunch, dinner daily

Eastern Cape

East London
La Villa Italiana (££–£££)
Restaurant with authentic Italian food – excellent veal carpaccio and other meat dishes, gnocchi and pastas.
✉ 42 Chamberlain Road ☎ 043-726 8162 🕐 Dinner daily

Quarterdeck (£–££)
Up-market pub and restaurant with a nautical theme, relaxed atmosphere and good food. Specialises in seafood and steaks.
✉ Orient Pavilion, Esplanade ☎ 043-743 5312 🕐 Lunch Mon–Fri; dinner Mon–Sat

Port Elizabeth
Blackbeard's Seafood Tavern (££–£££)
The restaurant enjoys a beautiful view out over King's Beach. Good seafood is the order of the day – calamari, oysters, fresh linefish – but there is also a selection of dishes for non-seafood eaters.
✉ Brooke's Pavilion, Beachfront ☎ 041-584 0691 🕐 Dinner Mon–Sat

Mauro's (££–£££)
The menu here at Mauro's offers a good range of both Italian and Mediterranean dishes along with general cuisine.
✉ Restaurant One, McArthur Bath Complex, Beach Road ☎ 041-582 2700/582 4910 🕐 Lunch, dinner daily

Graaff-Reinet
Andries Stockenstrom (££)
(Residents only, but highly recommended.) Restaurant in an old Cape cottage, with thick walls and lots of yellowwood furnishings. The regularly changing menu features dishes such as smoked kudu, marinated venison or guinea fowl; also good vegetarian dishes.
✉ 100 Cradock Street ☎ 049-892 4575 🕐 (Residents only) Dinner Mon–Sat

Grahamstown
The Monkey Puzzle Restaurant (££)
The Monkey Puzzle serves a wide variety of traditional Eastern Cape and South African dishes. It specialises in game dishes: ostrich, smoked springbok and kudu. In a beautiful setting in the botanical gardens.
✉ Lucas Avenue, Botanical Gardens ☎ 046-622 5318 🕐 Lunch Sat–Sun; dinner Wed–Mon

Northeast Region

KwaZulu-Natal

Durban
Bean Bag Bohemia (££)
Good food in a mellow atmosphere. There's a separate bar area downstairs serving light meals, and a formal restaurant upstairs. Try the avocado *mille-feuille* or rabbit with ginger.
✉ 18 Windermere Road, Greyville ☎ 031-309 6019
🕐 Lunch, dinner daily

Little India (£)
With cooks from both North and South India, this restaurant offers a full range of Indian dishes, including excellent biryanis and Tandoori chicken.
✉ 155 Musgrave Road, Musgrave ☎ 031-201 1121
🕐 Lunch, dinner daily

Il Cortile (££)
Relaxed trattoria with authentic décor. Italian food, from the staple pizzas and pastas to more varied vegetable dishes.
✉ 41 Marriot Road, Greyville ☎ 031-309 4160 🕐 Lunch, dinner Tue–Sun. Closed Sat lunch

The Edward Smorgasbord (££–£££)
This fabulous buffet, with a full range of seafood, is a Durban institution; set in the beautiful old, wood-panelled Chartroom of a traditional hotel.
✉ Edward Hotel, 149 Marine Parade ☎ 031-337 3681 🕐 Dinner Mon–Sat

Sala-Thai (££)
Tasty authentic Thai food, although the décor is not particularly eastern. The crispy chicken with chilli oyster sauce is especially good.
✉ 18 Old Main Road, Botha's Hill ☎ 031-765 5419 🕐 Lunch Sun; dinner Tue–Sat

Yorgo's Taverna (££)
Indoor or courtyard dining at this Greek restaurant serving traditional Greek specialities as well as Mediterranean pasta and seafood dishes.
✉ 200 Florida Road, Morningside ☎ 031-303 6375
🕐 Lunch Wed–Fri; dinner Mon–Sat

Umhlanga Rocks
Razzmatazz (££–£££)
The restaurant's wooden deck has a fine view of the beach and passing bathers, while the menu offers South African and excellent seafood specialities. Try the fish curry or the crocodile kebabs.
✉ Cabana Beach Resort, 10 Lagoon Drive ☎ 031-561 5847
🕐 Lunch, dinner daily

Pietermaritzberg
Turtle Bay (££)
The cuisine at this fun venue is mixed Mediterranean, Cajun and creole style. Dishes include prawns in tequila and lime, chicken breast stuffed with spinach and fillet of beef in red wine and mushrooms.
✉ Wembley Terrace, off Howick Road ☎ 033-394 5390
🕐 Lunch Tue–Fri; dinner Mon–Sat

Midlands
Old Halliwell (££)
This charming country inn offers outdoor dining in summer and roaring fires in winter. Excellent international and local dishes make up the small but

Beverages
Some South African restaurants – particularly those in the lower price range – have been a little slow to improve the quality of their beverages. Coffee, unless otherwise specified, may mean instant rather than filter. And so-called 'fresh' fruit juices are quite often made from concentrate containing preservatives. If in doubt, ask.

Waitrons

Your restaurant menu, or the manager, may refer to your 'waitron', but don't expect to be waited on by some sort of mechanised device. The term was invented by someone who wanted to save space and not to be gender-specific when advertising for staff. The word appeared in South Africa recently and seems to have caught on.

choice à la carte menu.

✉ Curry's Post ☎ 033-330 2602 🕐 Breakfast, lunch and dinner Tue–Sun

Mpumalanga

Dullstroom
The Poacher (££)

This traditional Scottish-style hostelry serves country fare and pub food. The menu includes butternut soup, various trout dishes, rabbit and game pies, and Kassler rib (smoked pork chop).

✉ Dullstroom ☎ 013-254 0108 🕐 Lunch, dinner Mon–Sat

Hazyview/White River
Highgrove House Restaurant (£££)

Intimate, candlelit restaurant with Anglo-French gourmet food and impeccable service. One of the country's best.

✉ On R40, between Hazyview and White River ☎ 013-764 1844 🕐 Breakfast, lunch and dinner daily by appointment only

Nelspruit
Le Gourmet (££–£££)

Quiet, up-market restaurant, but reasonably priced, and the best in town. Serves Gallic dishes and seafood from Mozambique in a lovely garden with lots of bird life.

✉ Corner of Voortrekker and Branders streets ☎ 013-755 1941 🕐 Lunch Tue–Sat; dinner Tue–Sun

Pilgrim's Rest
Mount Sheba Hotel (£££)

Memorable five-course dinner menu, including local panfried trout, duck and smoked ostrich with cranberries. Excellent wines.

✉ Pilgrim's Rest ☎ 013-768 1241 🕐 Breakfast, lunch, dinner daily

Sabie
The Woodsman (££)

Apart from panoramic views, this restaurant offers Greek-Cypriot cuisine as well as steaks, grills and pub food.

✉ 94 Main Road ☎ 013-764 2204 🕐 Breakfast, lunch, dinner daily

Zeederberg Coach House (£–££)

Pleasant family restaurant with a good basic menu of steaks, pasta, schnitzel and excellent German patisserie.

✉ Sabie ☎ 013-737 8101 🕐 Breakfast, dinner daily

White River
Cybele Forest Lodge (£££)

This elegant award-winning restaurant serves a range of international dishes, with local specialities such as ostrich carpaccio.

✉ 26km outside White River, on R40 towards Hazyview ☎ 013-764 1823 🕐 Breakfast, lunch, dinner daily

Northern Province

Louis Trichardt
Bergwater Restaurant (££)

Wonderful selection of seafood and traditional South African dishes.

✉ 5 Rissik Street ☎ 015-516 5774 🕐 Lunch, dinner Tue–Sun

Pholokwane (Pietersburg)
The Restaurant (££)

This restaurant in a Victorian house offers a variety of good food, ranging from Thai stir-fries to crepes with spinach and feta filling.

✉ 50 Dorp Street ☎ 015-291 1918 🕐 Lunch Mon–Fri; dinner Mon–Sat

Tzaneen
The Coach House (£££)

Housed in an old coaching inn, amid beautiful mountain scenery, the restaurant serves fine country fare, using local ingredients.

✉ Agatha Road, near Tzaneen ☎ 015-306 8000 🕐 Breakfast, lunch, dinner daily

Gauteng

Johannesburg

Assaggi (££)

The kitchen is an integral part of the dining experience at this charming Italian restaurant. Fabulous homemade pastas and carpaccio on offer.

✉ Illovo Post Office Centre ☎ 011-268 1370 🕔 Lunch Mon–Sat; dinner Mon–Fri

Le Canard (££)

Offers a choice of eating indoors or al fresco on the terrace. Try the delicious sauces with duck, seafood or venison. Good range of wines.

✉ 163 Rivonia Road, Morningside, Sandton ☎ 011-884 4597 🕔 Lunch Mon–Fri; dinner Mon–Sat

Chaplins (££–£££)

Cosy venue, specialising in low-fat tasty dishes of aubergine, prawns, ham, pasta and olives. The menu is also available in braille.

✉ 85 Fourth Avenue, Melville ☎ 011-482 4657 🕔 Lunch Mon–Fri; dinner Mon–Sat

Gatrile (£££)

Long-established, quality restaurant, serving dishes such as ostrich tartare, langoustine panzerotti, onion soup, soufflé and pickled beef pot au feu. Offers estate wines and cigars.

✉ 5 Esterhuyzen Street, Sandown ☎ 011-883 7399 🕔 Lunch Mon–Fri; dinner Tue–Sat

Gramadoelas (££)

Interesting eclectic African décor. The restaurant specialises in South African cuisine, particularly Cape Malay. Traditional fare such as mopani worms and crocodile also on offer.

✉ Market Theatre Complex ☎ 011-838 6960 🕔 Lunch Tue–Sat; dinner Mon–Sat

Ile de France (£££)

One of the city's premier restaurants, with excellent French cuisine. Top French chef and owner, specialising in soufflés.

✉ Cramerview Centre, 227 Main Road, Bryanston ☎ 011-706 2837 🕔 Lunch Sun–Fri; dinner daily

Lien Wah (££)

Chinese restaurant with Cantonese food; extremely reasonable five-course set menu on offer.

✉ Rosebank Hotel, Tyrwhitt Avenue ☎ 011-447 2700 🕔 Dinner Mon–Sat

Mary-Anne's Wholefood Emporium (£)

The name suggests the style of food: organic, preservative-free and vegetarian, including fresh soups, wholewheat bread, polenta, couscous, a variety of quiches, and unusual ice creams.

✉ The Colony Centre, 345 Jan Smuts Avenue ☎ 011-784 1930 🕔 Breakfast, lunch, dinner Mon–Sat

Piccolo Mondo (£££)

Fine ornate dining-room with piazza views. The executive chef and his team use only the freshest ingredients to produce outstanding Italian and international dishes.

✉ Michelangelo Hotel, Sandton Square, Sandton ☎ 011-282 7069 🕔 Lunch, dinner daily

Pomegranate (£££)

This restaurant, accommodated in a

Well-cooked Meat

South Africa produces excellent beef, lamb, pork, ostrich and poultry; mutton and veal, though available, are somewhat rarer. In general the locals prefer their meat reasonably well done, so what is called 'medium rare' here might be regarded as 'well done' elsewhere, and 'well done' might be thought 'overdone'. If you are very particular about the way your meat is cooked, explain this clearly to the waiter.

Cafés

You will see many outlets called 'cafés' around the country, but don't go in expecting to sit down, drink coffee, eat cake and read the papers. A 'café' in South African parlance means a corner store selling cigarettes, cool drinks (soft drinks), small groceries, magazines and newspapers – the equivalent of a British newsagent or corner shop, or American 7–11.

converted warehouse, has an eclectic menu with specialities such as puréed parsnip soup, salad with kiwifruit and fennel, Thai seafood, nasi goreng, and tomato tart.

> ✉ 79 Third Avenue, Melville
> ☎ 011-482 2366
> 🕐 Lunch Mon–Fri, dinner Mon–Sat

Sant' Anna (£££)

No pizzas at this up-market Italian restaurant, but you will find a range of delicious starters, and pasta made fresh on the premises.

> ✉ Dunkeld West Centre
> ☎ 011-341 0840 🕐 Lunch Sun–Fri; dinner Mon–Sat

Saxon Hotel (£££)

Impressive fortress-like building houses a restaurant serving international cuisine with an Afro-Asian accent, and sushi. The menu changes from summer to winter.

> ✉ 36 Saxon Road, Sandhurst
> ☎ 011-292 6000 🕐 Breakfast, lunch and dinner daily

Vilamoura (£££)

This relaxed Portuguese bistro specialises in seafood platters, but also does a range of Portuguese national dishes.

> ✉ Corner of Fifth and Alice streets ☎ 011-884 0360
> 🕐 Lunch Mon–Fri; dinner Mon–Sat

Pretoria

Brasserie de Paris (££)

At the Brasserie de Paris you'll find beautifully presented French food in an intimate atmosphere. There is a varied menu, including pork fillet with prunes and roast guinea-fowl, and a well-

selected wine list.

> ✉ 525 Duncan Street, Hatfield
> ☎ 012-362 2247 🕐 Lunch Mon–Fri; dinner Mon–Sat

Die Werf (££)

Die Werf offers South African cuisine in a country setting, set amid attractive gardens. The menu includes typical local dishes and a choice of unusual specialities such as curried mutton tripe.

> ✉ Plot 66, Olympus Drive, Pretoria East ☎ 012-991 1809
> 🕐 Lunch Tue–Sun; dinner Tue–Sat

Mostapha's (££)

A Moroccan restaurant, serving chicken, beef meatballs, lamb and fish, with couscous. There is a small wine list and expect to pay a R8 corkage charge if you decide bring your own wine.

> ✉ 478 Duncan Street, Hatfield
> ☎ 012-432 3855 🕐 Lunch and dinner daily

Pachas (££)

Colourful interior, wall-papered with menus. Interesting mix of dishes, such as smoked duck breast, lobster bisque and ostrich kebabs; also outstanding steaks.

> ✉ Club R Shopping Centre, 22 Dely Road, Hazelwood
> ☎ 012-460 0003 🕐 Lunch Mon–Fri; dinner Mon–Sat

La Perla (££)

This is an elegant, up-market restaurant offering a choice of Continental cuisine ranging from pâté de foie gras to frogs' legs.

> ✉ On the corner of Bronkhorst and Tram streets ☎ 012-460 1267 🕐 Lunch and dinner Mon–Sat

Northwest Region

Bethlehem
The Wooden Spoon (£–££)
Housed in the oldest building in town, this restaurant and pub offers simple, good quality food: *biltong* (dried meat) salad, pork dishes, seafood, and delicious home-made bread.

✉ **12 Church Street** ☎ **058-303 2724** ⏰ **Lunch, teas, dinner Mon–Sat**

Bloemfontein
Beef Baron (££)
Steakhouse with a variety of cuts of meat on the menu, served with an interesting range of sauces – bone marrow and bacon, or spinach and feta cheese. Seafood also available. Comprehensive wine list.

✉ **22 Second Avenue** ☎ **051-447 4290** ⏰ **Lunch Tue–Fri, dinner Mon–Sat**

Berghof (££)
This Italian-style villa houses a restaurant where French and Italian cuisine is on offer, including unusual dishes like quail and kumquat consommé, and butternut and ricotta in seaweed. Small, select wine list.

✉ **Eeufees Road Extension, near Noordstad Centre** ☎ **051-433 1944** ⏰ **Lunch buffet Sun; dinner Mon–Sat**

Onze Rust (££)
Restaurant situated on an old family farm, offering traditional Afrikaner food prepared to a high culinary standard, using the freshest local ingredients. The historic bar has Boer War memorabilia.

✉ **18km south of Bloemfontein, off the N1** ☎ **051-443 8717** ⏰ **Breakfast, lunch, dinner daily by appointment only**

Ladybrand
Cranberry Cottage (£–££)
Set in a traditional Free State sandstone house, the restaurant offers a set menu with a choice for each course. Delicious, unpretentious food and good value for money.

✉ **37 Beeton Street** ☎ **051-924 2290** ⏰ **Breakfast, teas, dinner daily**

Welkom
Siete's Restaurant (££)
Well-established restaurant, serving mainly meat and seafood dishes, though vegetarian options are also available. Try the blackened Cajun chicken, or flamed pork fillet with spinach and feta.

✉ **17 Mooi Street** ☎ **057-352 6539** ⏰ **Lunch Tue–Fri, dinner Mon–Sat**

Northwest

Sun City (£–£££)
A large variety of food outlets is available here at Sun City (there are 28 in all), offering the whole range from economy fast-food at Nando's to *haute cuisine* at the Villa del Palazzo. Something to suit all tastes and pockets.

✉ **Sun City** ☎ **014-557 1000** ⏰ **Breakfast, lunch, dinner daily**

Northern Cape

Upington
Le Must Restaurant (££)
Le Must is the best restaurant in town, serving good local and international dishes accompanied by excellent service.

✉ **11 Schröder Street** ☎ **054-332 3971** ⏰ **Daily**

Unusual Drinks
Visitors to South Africa may be unfamiliar with some of the local alcoholic drinks. Quite popular are several types of liqueur, flavoured with indigenous fruits, such as the amarula berry, with added cream for smoothness (their names often contain the words 'velvet', or 'cream'). There are a number of other varieties of potent, locally distilled alcohol (some of doubtful legality), such as *mampoer* (home-distilled brandy), or *witblits* (white lightning).

Western & Eastern Cape

Prices

Approximate prices are based on high season, double room, per person sharing. Some hotels are willing to negotiate on price.

£ = under 200 Rand
££ = 200–500 Rand
£££ = over 500 Rand

Western Cape

Cape Town

The Cape Castle (££)

All-suite hotel, close to the Victoria and Alfred Waterfront (➤ 26); very secure and good value for this location. The suites are luxurious, with satellite TV and air-conditioning; swimming-pool.

✉ 3 Main Road, Green Point
☎ 021-439 1016; fax: 021-439 1019; www.castles.co.za

Cape Gardens Lodge Hotel (££)

Very centrally located, right next to the Company's Garden (➤ 34) and close to the city centre. À la carte restaurants; some rooms with mountain view. Air-conditioning.

✉ 88 Queen Victoria Street
☎ 021-423 1260;
fax: 021-423 2088;
www.capegardenslodge.co.za

Cape Swiss Hotel (££)

Just outside the city centre, with a large variety of restaurants and shops within walking distance. The exterior may be unprepossessing, but the rooms are elegant. There's a popular pub downstairs, as well as a restaurant on the first floor.

✉ Corner of Kloof and Camp streets ☎ 021-423 4402;
e-mail:
capeswiss@fortesking_hotels.co.za

Hotel Graeme (£)

A small, modest hotel, but well situated and excellent value for money. Within walking distance of the Victoria and Alfred Waterfront (➤ 26) and close to the city centre. Self-catering family rooms with their own kitchen facilities also available.

✉ 107 Main Road, Green Point
☎ 021-434 9282; fax: 021-434 9283; e-mail:
graeme@mweb.co.za

Mount Nelson (£££)

Arguably the country's most prestigious hotel, frequented by royalty and celebrities alike. Beautiful colonial-style building set in lush gardens, at the head of the Company's Garden (➤ 34), close to the city centre and museums.

✉ 76 Orange Street ☎ 021-483 1000; fax: 021-483 7472

Park Inn (£££)

Right in the centre of town, within walking distance of the historic heart of the city and many restaurants and nightclubs. Situated on Cape Town's famous Greenmarket Square (➤ 34).

✉ 10 Greenmarket Square, PO Box 1215 ☎ 021-423 2050;
fax: 021-423 2059

Table Mountain Lodge (££)

Well-appointed guest house with excellent views of Table Mountain and the city. Within easy reach of the city centre and major tourist attractions, but without the noise and crowds. Comfortable rooms, individually decorated.

✉ 10A Tamboerskloof Road
☎ 021-423 0042; fax: 021-423 4983;
www.tablemountainlodge.co.za

Vineyard (££–£££)

An excellent, up-market hotel with spectacular mountain views, set in exquisite gardens leading down to the Liesbeeck River. Gourmet restaurant, Au Jardin (➤ 92), heated pool and gym.

🖾 **Colinton Road, Newlands**
☎ **021-683 3044; fax: 021-683 3365**

Winchester Mansions Hotel (£££)

Pleasantly situated on the Sea Point esplanade, overlooking the Atlantic Ocean, this hotel offers good value for money. Just a few minutes drive from the main tourist attraction of the city.

🖾 **221 Beach Road, Sea Point**
☎ **021-434 2351; fax: 021-434 0215; e-mail: sales@winchester.co.za**

Franschhoek
Franschhoek Country House (££)

This restored manor house, set in tranquil gardens, was once a perfumery. Rooms feature handcrafted furniture and many have their own private patios; swimming pool and excellent French restaurant.

🖾 **Main Road** ☎ **021-876 3386; fax: 021-876 2744; www.ecl.co.za**

Knysna
Leisure Isle Lodge (££)

Guest house on Leisure Island in the Knysna Lagoon. All rooms are en suite; there is swimming in a heated pool or the lagoon itself; in-house pub.

🖾 **87 Bayswater Drive, Leisure Isle** ☎ **044-384 0462; fax: 044-384 1027; www.lodgeview@mweb.co.za**

Matjiesfontein
Lord Milner Hotel (£–££)

The whole village of Matjiesfontein, including this gracious Victorian hotel, has been declared a national monument. The old coffee house and pub are also worth a visit.

🖾 **Logan Road** ☎ **023-551 3011; fax: 023-551 3020; www.matjiesfontein.com**

Montagu
Montagu Rose (£–££)

Pretty guest house in the heart of Montagu; relaxing and private atmosphere. The staff are welcoming and there is a wonderful home-made breakfast buffet. Not far from Montagu hot springs (➤ 43).

🖾 **19 Kohler Street** ☎ **023-614 2681; fax: 023-614 2780**

Mossel Bay
Huijs te Marquette (££)

This hotel offers 12 finely decorated en suite rooms; three lounge areas; private bar; bed-and-breakfast, with dinner on request; swimming pool.

🖾 **1 Marsh Street** ☎ **044-691 3182 (also fax); e-mail: marquette@pixie.co.za**

Paarl
Oak Tree Lodge (££)

The lodge has spectacular views of the vineyards and Paarl Mountain, with cosy en suite rooms. Near the Paarl winelands and numerous hiking trails. Swimming pool.

🖾 **32 Main Street** ☎ **021-863 2631; fax: 021-863 2607; www.oaktreelodge.co.za**

Stellenbosch
Stellenbosch Hotel (££–£££)

Beautiful hotel in an original Cape Dutch-style building. The staff are friendly and the hotel has a good seafood restaurant. Well located for

Accommodation

In recent years, with the huge growth of tourism to South Africa, bed-and-breakfast establishments and guest houses have sprung up all over the country, so much so that even without booking in advance you can generally find a place to stay. Phone ahead to the tourist office of the next town you will be visiting to secure excellent, reasonably priced accommodation.

Hotel Staff

Hotel personnel – chambermaids, porters, doormen – are not paid particularly well in South Africa, so, if you can, tip generously when leaving. Also, if you establish a personal relationship by talking to the staff – telling them about yourself and where you come from, and asking about them and their families – you will find that levels of service often improve dramatically.

sightseeing in Stellenbosch's historical district, and a good base for the local wine route.

✉ Corner of Dorp and Andringa streets ☎ 021-887 3644; fax: 021-887 3673; e-mail: stbhotel@mweb.co.za

Swellendam
Swellengrebel Hotel (££)
Comfortable luxury rooms available at this hotel en route from Cape Town to the Garden Route.

✉ 91 Voortrekker Street ☎ 02851-41144; fax: 02851-42453; e-mail: swellen@sdm.doria.co.za

Garden Route

Knysna
Knysna Log-Inn (££)
Just a few hundred metres from the waterfront and the town centre. Unusual wooden hotel with a striking glassed front. Offers twin rooms or loft suites, swimming pool, jacuzzi and sauna.

✉ 16 Gray Street ☎ 044-382 5835; fax: 044-382 5830; www.cli.co.za

Oudtshoorn
Protea Hotel Riempie Estate (££)
Good accommodation situated near the centre of town and the historic sights and museums.

✉ Baron van Rheede Street ☎ 044-272 6161; fax: 044-272 6772; e-mail: ostrich@pixie.co.za

Plettenberg Bay
Fynbos Ridge Cottages (££)
These self-catering, exclusive Cape-style cottages are set amid beautiful surroundings.

✉ Plettenberg Bay ☎ 044-532 7862 (also fax); www.fynbosridge.co.za

Eastern Cape

East London
Esplanade (££)
Affordable hotel in a good location right on the main beachfront. Special rates available for children under the age of 16.

✉ 6 Clifford Street, Quigney, Beachfront ☎ 043-722 2518; fax: 043-722 5375; e-mail: esphotel@iafrica.com

Port Elizabeth
Beach Hotel (PE) (££)
On the beachfront, near the dolphinarium and close to the shopping centre. Safe swimming, surfing and sailing. Veranda restaurant serving light meals and cocktails. Ample parking.

✉ Marine Drive ☎ 041-583 2161; fax: 041-583 6220; e-mail: reservations@pehotels.co.za

Graaff-Reinet
Drostdy Hotel (££–£££)
An elegant, old-world hotel with impeccable service and a comfortable atmosphere. Centrally located.

✉ 30 Church Street ☎ 049-892 2161; fax: 049-892 4582; e-mail: drosdy@intekom.co.za

Grahamstown
Protea Hotel Grahamstown (££–£££)
Offers all the facilities and reliable service you would expect from a well-established hotel chain with an in-house family and an à la carte restaurant, as well as a bar.

✉ 123 High Street ☎ 046-622 2366; fax: 046-622 2424; e-mail: grahotel@intekom.co.za

Northeast Region

Durban

Albany Hotel (£–££)
Situated in the heart of Durban, this hotel offers air-conditioned en suite rooms with TV, restaurant and pub.
 225 Smith Street ☎ 031-304 4381; fax: 031-307 1411; e-mail: albany@iafrica.com

Blue Waters Hotel (££)
Long-established hotel, on the beachfront, offering reasonably priced spacious, en suite rooms with private balcony. Undercover parking.
✉ 175 Snell Parade ☎ 031-332 4272; fax: 031-337 5817; e-mail: bluewater@eca.co.za

City Lodge Durban (££)
Close to the main Durban attractions. Spacious, comfortable rooms. Secure parking and swimming pool.
✉ Corner of Brickhill and Old Fort roads ☎ 031-332 1447; fax: 031-332 1483; www.citylodge.co.za

Durban Morningside Lodge (£)
On the slopes above the city, slightly away from the centre of town, offering 44 rooms, with guest house restaurant.
✉ 186 Innes Road, Morningside ☎ 031-312 2236 e-mail: morningside@saol.com

Essenwood House (££)
Fine accommodation overlooking the city and ocean; close to shopping mall. Five air-conditioned, en suite, double rooms, swimming pool and parking.
✉ 630 Essenwood Road ☎ 031-207 4547 (and fax); e-mail: info@essenwoodhouse.co.za

Holiday Inn Garden Court Marine Parade (££)
Convenient and reasonably priced, on the beachfront. The Garden Grill restaurant serves breakfast and dinner.
✉ 167 Marine Parade ☎ 031-337 3341; fax: 031-337 5929; www.southernsun.com

Parade Hotel (£)
Opposite swimming-pool and North Beach. Rooms have a sea view and bath; breakfast included in price.
✉ 191 Marine Parade ☎ 031-337 4565; fax: 031-332 0251; email: paradehotel@eca.co.za

Royal Hotel (££–£££)
Impressive and stylish hotel. Luxurious rooms and suites are decorated in warm yellowwood and the bathrooms in marble. Choice of restaurants.
✉ 267 Smith Street ☎ 031-304 0331; fax: 031-307 6884; www.theroyal.co.za

Pietermaritzburg & The Midlands

Imperial Protea (££)
Centrally located, historic hotel with elegant rooms and spacious surroundings. Bar and restaurant in house.
✉ 224 Loop Street, Pietermaritzburg ☎ 033-342 6551; fax: 033-342 9796; e-mail: imperial@iafrica.com

Umhlanga Rocks

Burgundy Bay House (££)
African-Mediterranean-style guest house, 50m from the beach, provides personal service; swimming pool and help with golfing itineraries.
✉ PO Box 1024, Umhlanga Rocks ☎ 031-562 9986 (also fax); www.burgundybay.co.za

Oyster Box (££)
Long-established, elegant, comfortable hotel with own swimming pool and well-

Touring by train
If you are not in a hurry, long-distance travel by train is a wonderful, and relatively inexpensive, way to be accommodated and see the country at the same time. It is best to book first-class. You will be brought bedding by a steward, and can have all your meals in an old-fashioned dining-car.

Budget Holidays

Budget travellers are well catered for in South Africa. There are good camping and caravanning sites in all areas, including many National Parks. Some sites have only basic facilities, but many offer washing blocks, cooking areas and a swimming pool. In the cities and main tourist areas many backpacking lodges have opened in recent years.

known restaurant, the Oyster Box. Close to beach.
✉ 2 Lighthouse Road ☎ 031-561 2233; fax: 031-561 4072

Drakensberg
Cathedral Peak Hotel (££)
Accommodation of a high standard in the heart of the Drakensberg. Swimming, squash, horse riding, hiking.
✉ Cathedral Peak, Drakensberg ☎ 036-488 1888; fax: 036-488 1889

The Nest (££)
Relaxed country lodge in an old colonial building. Veranda overlooking the pool, views of the Central Drakensberg.
✉ Private Bag X14, Winterton 3340 ☎ 036-468 1068; fax: 036-468 1390; www.thenest.co.za

Mpumalanga

Hazyview
Chestnut Country Lodge (£)
Quiet country guest house in beautiful gardens with spectacular mountain views. Near to Blyde River Canyon (➤ 16), and Numbi Gate of Kruger (➤ 22–3). No children under the age of 12.
✉ PO Box 156, Kiepersol 1241 ☎ 013-737 8195; fax: 013-737 8196; www.chestnutlodge.co.za

Farmhouse Country Lodge (££)
Near to the attractions of the area, this country house hotel offers a swimming pool, horse riding and hiking.
✉ 40km north of Nelspruit on Hazyview road ☎ 013-737 8780; fax: 013-737 8783

Kruger National Park Restcamps (££)
Restcamps, run by the National Parks Board, with communal kitchen facilities, restaurant, barbecue area. Hiking, holiday programmes and wildlife film shows offered at many camps. Book well in advance.

☎ 012-428 9111; e-mail: reservations@parks-sa.co.za

Sabi River Sun (££–£££)
Safari hotel on the banks of the Sabi River, with thatched buildings set amid bushveld. Barbecues are held in the boma (reeded enclosure) overlooking the river. Game drives into nearby Sabi Sand Reserve and Kruger.
✉ PO Box 13, Hazyview 1242 ☎ 013-737 7311; fax: 013-737 7314; e-mail: lettishas@southernsun.com

Barberton
Diggers Retreat (££)
Owner-run hotel just outside Barberton. Gold-panning and trips to Eureka City arranged. Ideal stop-over for Kruger.
✉ Main Street, Noord Kaap ☎ 013-719 9681; fax: 013-719 9684

Pilgrim's Rest
Royal Hotel (££)
Beautifully restored 19th-century buildings, now a national monument. Elegant rooms with Victorian-style furnishings.
✉ PO Box 59, Pilgrims Rest 1290 ☎ 013-768 1100; e-mail: royal@mweb.co.za

Northern Province

Phalaborwa
Tulani Safari Lodge (£££)
Luxurious thatched lodge in the heart of elephant country, within easy reach of the surrounding game.
✉ PO Box 148, Phalaborwa 1398 ☎ 015-781 5414; fax: 015-769 6065; www.tulanisafarilodge.co.za

Soutpansberg
Clouds End Hotel (£)
Quiet hotel in the foothills of the Soutpansberg Mountains; swimming pool.
✉ Private Bag 2409, Louis Trichardt, 7920 ☎ 015-517 7021; fax: 015-517 7187; e-mail: cloudsend@mweb.co.za

Gauteng

Johannesburg
Cullinan Inn (££–£££)
Set in up-market Sandton, just north of the city centre. Luxurious, but not exorbitantly priced. Pleasant à la carte restaurant and cocktail bar; swimming pool.

✉ **1 Cullinan Close, Morningside, Sandton** ☎ **011-884 1804; fax: 011-884 6040; e-mail: higcjhbmorningside@southernsun.com**

The Melville Turret Guest House (£–££)
Set in a beautiful, turreted old house in a quiet suburb. Near to popular 7th Street and its restaurants, nightclubs and cafés.

✉ **Corner of 2nd Avenue and 9th Street, Melville** ☎ **011-482 7197; fax: 011-482 5725**

Park Hyatt (£££)
In the fashionable suburb of Rosebank, close to the shops and restaurants. Cocktail terrace, excellent restaurant. Wine bar features nightly live music.

✉ **PO Box 1536, Saxonwold 2132** ☎ **011-280 1234; fax: 011-280 1238; e-mail: parkhyatt@icon.co.za**

The Parktonian (££–£££)
Centrally located hotel, opposite the Civic Theatre; many restaurants and other places of entertainment near by. Sauna and heated swimming pool.

✉ **120 De Korte Street, Braamfontein** ☎ **011-403 5740; fax: 011-403 2401; e-mail: accom@park.co.za**

Waybury House (££)
Bed-and-breakfast guest house offering a personal touch. Rates include dinner.

✉ **Sandton** ☎ **011-886 6898; fax: 011-886 6896**

Magaliesberg
Sparkling Waters (££)
Country hotel with 56 rooms, all with air-conditioning, en suite bathroom and TV. The hotel offers swimming, horse riding and mini-golf.

✉ **Between Rustenburg and Magaliesberg (map on web site)** ☎ **014-535 0000/1/2; fax: 014-535 0007; www.sparklingwaters.co.za**

Pretoria
Holiday Inn Garden Court (££)
Comfortable, centrally situated hotel, within walking distance of the main attractions. Restaurants; outdoor swimming pool.

✉ **Corner of Minnaar and Van der Walt streets** ☎ **012-322 7500; fax: 012-322 9429; e-mail: hotel@burgerspark.co.za**

Park Gables (£–££)
Guest house with 12 spacious en suite bedrooms; near to Pretoria Art Museum.

✉ **784 Park Street, Arcadia** ☎ **012-344 0390; fax: 012-344 5643; www.parkgables.co.za**

Pretoria Hof Hotel (££)
Right in the heart of the city, next to the State Theatre, this hotel offers comfort at reasonable rates; restaurant.

✉ **295 Pretorius Street** ☎ **012-322 7570; fax: 012-322 9461; e-mail: phho@global.co.za**

Victoria Hotel (£££)
Luxury hotel offers elegant rooms, decorated in original Victorian style, an excellent restaurant and its own pub.

✉ **Corner of Scheiding and Paul Kruger streets** ☎ **012-323 6054; fax: 324-2426**

Township stays
A new local phenomenon is the availability of bed-and-breakfasts in some of the townships and shack-settlements that fringe all the main urban centres. These give you a chance to experience the conditions in which many South Africans live. Contact the Tourism Offices in Cape Town, Durban or Johannesburg for details (► 120).

Northwest Region

Beautiful B&Bs
Some of the most beautiful and relatively inexpensive accommodation can be found in guest houses and bed-and-breakfasts in the small towns and on farms in the rural areas. Often the buildings are Victorian or older, and the rooms are furnished with interesting old-fashioned pieces. Information about such places is sometimes hard to come by; ask locally, or follow the signs by the side of the road.

Free State

Bloemfontein
De Oude Kraal Country Estate (££)
Relax under the blue gums on this farm just outside Bloemfontein. Has traditional farm cooking, its own pub, cosy accommodation, swimming and riding.
✉ Tierpoort, 35km south of Bloemfontein; PO Box 35245, Faunasig 9325 ☎ 051-564 0636; fax: 051-564 4635; e-mail: deoude@intekom.co.za

Protea Hotel Bloemfontein (££)
Has the inevitable sameness of a chain hotel, but with the advantage of being centrally situated, near the historic sights.
✉ PO Box 2212, Bloemfontein ☎ 051-403 8000; fax: 051-447 7102

Ladybrand
Cranberry Cottage (££)
Antique-filled guest house; pretty garden with duck pond. Ideal base to visit Lesotho (➤ 90) and the many Bushman rock paintings in the area. Offers horse riding and hiking.
✉ 37 Beeton Street ☎ 051-924 2290; fax: 051-924 1168; e-mail: crancott@xsinet.co.za

Northwest Province

Sun City (££–£££)
➤ 87

Bakubung (£££)
Located in the Pilanesberg Game Reserve (➤ 87), this resort offers luxurious rooms with views of the bushveld, outdoor barbecues, a natural rock swimming pool and game drives.

✉ PO Box 6805, Rustenburg 0300 ☎ 014-552 6000; e-mail: kfinney@legacyhotels.co.za

Northern Cape

Kimberley
Protea Hotel Diamond Lodge (££)
Situated in central Kimberley, just five minutes from the Big Hole (➤ 21). Comfortable, centrally heated rooms; a variety of restaurants near by.
✉ 124 Du Toitspan Road ☎ 0538-311281; fax: 0538-311284; e-mail: dplkim@global.co.za

Okiep
Okiep Country Hotel (££)
This comfortable country hotel, located right in the heart of Namaqualand, is an ideal base for viewing the spectacular spring flowers (➤ 24). Owner can advise about 4x4 and hiking trails.
✉ PO Box 17, Okiep 8270 ☎ 027-744 1000; fax: 027-744 1170; e-mail: okiep@intekom.co.za

Upington
Oasis Lodge (££)
Pleasant hotel with tropical plants and water features. Comfortable accommodation is reasonably priced and there is an in-house bar and a nearby steakhouse.
✉ PO Box 1981, Upington 8800 ☎ 054-337 8500; fax: 054-337 8599; www.protea_hotels.co.za; e-mail: upthotels@yebo.co.za

Protea Hotel (££)
The Protea has all the amenities you would expect in a good chain hotel: en suite rooms with TV, restaurants and a pub.
✉ 24 Schröder Street ☎ 054-337 8400; fax: 054-337 8499; e-mail: upthotels@yebo.co.za

Shopping in South Africa

Books & Music

Cape Town

Exclusive Books

This shop offers a huge range of quality books, including plenty on South Africa. Anything they don't have on the shelves they will order for you. This is part of a nationwide chain.

✉ 225 Victoria Wharf, Box 50105, Waterfront ☎ 021-419 0905

Look & Listen

Stocks a large range of CDs, with plenty of listening points to hear your chosen selection.

✉ 1st Floor, Cavendish Square, Claremont
☎ 021-683 1810

CNA

Stationery, paperbacks and a good selection of toys and music are on sale here. There are stores countrywide.

✉ Victoria Wharf, Victoria and Alfred Waterfront ☎ 021-418 3510

Durban

Juta

Large range of general interest and specialist books. Has outlets around the country.

✉ 216 Stanger Street
☎ 031-337 3970

Johannesburg

Musica

Here you'll find a large selection of CDs from a variety of genres. Has stores countrywide.

✉ Shop 101, Fourways Mall, Bryanston, Sandton ☎ 011-705 3579 (also fax); www.musica.co.za

Shopping Centres & Malls

Cape Town

Cavendish Square

This is an up-market shopping centre in the southern suburbs with a variety of speciality shops, clothes shops, food shops, boutiques, department stores, book shops and cinemas.

✉ Dreyer Street, Claremont
☎ 021-674 3050

Victoria & Alfred Waterfront

Large shopping complex (► 26) with numerous stores selling just about everything: arts and crafts, clothing, jewellery, curios, photographic equipment. You'll also find a supermarket, flea markets, many cinemas and eateries here.

☎ 021-408 7600

Tygervalley Centre

Large mall just outside Cape Town. Department stores, cinemas, restaurants, a supermarket, and a variety of speciality shops selling, among other things, camping equipment, clothing and crafts.

✉ Tygervalley Centre, Bezuidenhout Avenue, Bellville
☎ 021-914 1822

Durban

The Pavilion

This enormous, picturesque mall was built in the style of a Victorian conservatory. It offers a comprehensive range of shops.

✉ Spine Road, Westville, 10km west on the N3 from Durban city centre ☎ 031-265 0558

Shopping Hours

Shopping hours are generally from 8:30 or 9 until 4:30 or 5 on weekdays and until 12:30 or 1 on Saturdays. In small towns shops may shut for lunch. Most close on Saturday afternoon and Sunday. The big shopping malls in the major cities tend to be an exception, often having evening shopping, and remaining open on the weekend.

South African Writers
If you are looking for local fiction in English there is a wide range to choose from. Well-known authors include novelists Andre Brink, J M Coetzee (twice winner of the Booker Prize), Nobel laureate Nadine Gordimer, Ezekiel Mphahlele, Sol Plaatjie and Olive Schreiner (► 14); among the short-story writers, the best-known are Herman Charles Bosman (► 14) and Richard Rive.

Victoria Street Market
Large, covered, mainly Indian market with many small outlets; excellent for brasswear, fabrics and spices.
🖂 **Between Victoria and Queen streets** ☎ **031-305 3344**

The Wheel
Popular mall with a nautical theme just behind the beachfront, offering over 100 stores and 12 cinemas. A huge Ferris wheel gives the centre its name.
🖂 **55 Gillespie Street** ☎ **031-332 4324**

The Workshop
A smart complex in the city centre with a variety of shops and restaurants. It is situated in a converted Victorian railway workshop.
🖂 **Corner of Commercial and Aliwal streets, adjacent to Tourist Junction** ☎ **031-304 9894**

Johannesburg
Eastgate Shopping Mall
With 250 shops, this is one of the largest malls on the continent. There are clothing shops, department stores, cinemas, restaurants, interior shops and boutiques among others.
🖂 **43 Bradford Road, Bedford View** ☎ **011-616 2209**

Hyde Park Corner
Designer clothes shops, up-market international chains and speciality stores. Restaurants and cinemas.
🖂 **Corner of Jan Smuts and William Nicol, Hyde Park** ☎ **011-325 4340**

Oriental Plaza
This is a large, busy mall with many small shops; it is especially strong on spices, fabrics and cheap clothing.
🖂 **Fordsburg** ☎ **011-838 6752**

Rosebank Shopping Mall
Large range of fairly pricey designer shops, department stores, cinemas and restaurants.
🖂 **Jan Smuts Avenue, Rosebank**
☎ **011-788 5530**

Sandton Square and Sandton City
Huge up-market shopping complex joined by a galleria, incorporating two malls. Vast array of shops, restaurants and cinemas.
☎ **011-883 2011**

Randburg Waterfront
Here you'll find a great variety of shops, restaurants and entertainment in a beautiful waterfront setting (► 71).
🖂 **Corner of Republic Road and Hans Strydom Avenue, Randburg** ☎ **011-789 5052**

Pretoria
Hatfield Plaza Shopping Centre
Variety of stores, from books to clothing and gifts.
🖂 **1122 Burnett Street, Hatfield** ☎ **012-362 5842**

Arts, Crafts & Collectables

Cape Town
Clementina
Sells tableware and ornamental plates made and painted by some of the country's best-known ceramic artists; also various other crafts.
🖂 **20 Main Road, Kalk Bay**
☎ **021-788 8718**

Indaba Curios
Here at Indaba Curios you'll find a variety of African curios and collectables for sale.

✉ **Victoria and Alfred Waterfront** ☎ **021-425 3639**

Greenmarket Square
An ever-popular outdoor market in the city centre, with a wide variety of crafts and curios, as well as clothing and jewellery (➤ 34). Well woth a visit.

✉ **Greenmarket Square**

Green Point Flea Market
Huge Sunday flea market with everything from bric-à-brac to antiques and curios. Good bargain hunting.

✉ **Next to Green Point Stadium, Green Point** ⊙ **Sun**

St George's Mall
Pedestrian mall in the centre of Cape Town, with numerous arts and craft stalls, as well as curios and original artworks for sale.

✉ **St George's Mall**

Long Street
Well known for its antique and bric-a-brac shops. Lots of second-hand and vintage clothes and book stores (➤ 35).

Durban
Amphitheatre Craft Market
This is one of Durban's oldest markets. Especially good for textiles and curios; also ceramics, Indian and African clothes, handmade shoes.

✉ **Amphitheatre, North Beach**

The Bazaar
Wide range of goods on offer, including African curios and leather items.

✉ **Gillespie Street**

South Plaza Market
Hundreds of stalls with a huge variety of merchandise. Good for textiles, curios and collectables.

✉ **Aliwal Street, adjacent to the Durban Exhibition Centre** ☎ **031-301 9900** ⊙ **Sun**

Johannesburg
Art-Glass Studios
An outlet for stained glass and other glass objects; it also includes an exhibition space.

✉ **1 Long Avenue, Glenhazel, Johannesburg** ☎ **011-887 5876**

Firenze Gallery
This gallery creates and sells its own ceramics, stained glass and découpage works of art.

✉ **Beyers Naude Street Extension** ☎ **011-659 0034**

Mukondeni Art
Sells South African sculpture, pottery and functional art of outstanding quality. Recently won Gallery of the Year award.

✉ **36 Orleans Road, Kaya Sands** ☎ **011-708 2116**

Rooftop Market
Sunday market offering arts, crafts, antiques, African artefacts and live entertainment.

✉ **Rosebank Mall** ☎ **011-442 4488** ⊙ **Sun**

Randburg
Shades of Ngwenya
You can buy charming ornaments and animals here made from recycled glass.

✉ **Corner of Beyers Naude and Diepsloot roads, Johannesburg** ☎ **011-957 3180**

Recycled Art
Local artists and craftspeople are skilled at creating striking, often beautiful objects out of the most unpromising recycled materials. Look out for chickens made from folded and trimmed plastic rubbish bags; cars and earrings made from the metal of soft drink cans; and aeroplanes, cars, animals and fruit bowls made from galvanised wire.

Buying Locally
South Africans say 'Local is *lekker* (nice)'. If you want to follow this principle in your shopping, buy ceramics, jewellery and paintings in Cape Town; ostrich eggs and leather in Oudtshoorn; wooden articles along the Garden Route, especially around Knysna; curios, masks, beadwork and baskets in KwaZulu-Natal; and skins, painted cloth and batiks in Mpumalanga.

Children's Attractions

Children's Activities
With its generally fine dry climate, South Africa is an easy place to entertain children. At the coast, you can take them to the beach and let them build sandcastles or dabble in the rock pools. Inland you can turn them loose on the lawns of the botanical gardens, or take them to the funfair, the zoo or the public swimming pool. In many cities there are restaurants, such as the Spur chain, which welcome children and provide them with colouring-books and balloons.

Cape Town
Boulders Beach Penguins
The pretty beach has a colony of jackass penguins (➤ 40).
✉ Boulders Beach, south of Simon's Town

Mini Train
A miniature steam engine pulls passenger coaches along a circular small-gauge track with views of the sea and the lawns. Mini-golf is available alongside.
✉ Mouille Point, next to the lighthouse ☎ 021-434 8537 ⏰ Weekends and public holidays 11–6, weekdays by appointment

Ratanga Junction
South Africa's biggest theme park offers roller-coasters, water-rides, live entertainment, restaurants and cinemas.
✉ Off the N1, Sable road ☎ 021-550 8504; www.ratanga.co.za ⏰ Dec–Apr, Wed–Sun 10–5

Rhodes Memorial
Generations of children have enjoyed climbing all over the full-size bronze lions here; there is a tea room (➤ 42) right behind the memorial.
✉ Off Rhodes Drive, Groote Schuur Estate ⏰ Daylight hours

Scratch Patch
This outlet on the Victoria and Alfred Waterfront (➤ 26), which sells semi-precious stones, is like an Aladdin's Cave for children (and adults), where they can root around piles of inexpensive stones and select their own.
✉ Victoria and Alfred Waterfront

South African Museum
Good Discovery Room for children. Older ones will enjoy the Planetarium next door (➤ 38).

Two Oceans Aquarium
Has a section where children can handle shells and sea-creatures (➤ 39).

Garden Route
Outeniqua Choo Tjoe
This steam train runs daily from George to Knysna, pulling old-fashioned passenger coaches. The beautifully scenic route takes in beaches, woodlands and the spectacular Kaaimans River bridge crossing. Seven-hour round trip, including a two-hour stop in Knysna.
✉ Station Street, George ☎ 044-801 8288

Port Elizabeth
Algoa Grand Prix
Offers a fun, small-scale, racing experience, either on a 40m four-lane Scalextric track, or in 160cc go-karts. Helmets and balaclavas are provided.
✉ Badger Building, corner of Uitenhage and Somers roads, Sydenham ☎ 041-487 3981

Oceanarium
Port Elizabeth's popular Oceanarium offers entertaining seal and dolphin shows (➤ 47).

Durban
Golden Mile
This is paradise for children, offering beach, lawns, paddling pools, rides in boats and rickshaws, Minitown – a miniature city spread over 1.2ha, with buildings, trains moving on tracks and ships on miniature waterways –

ice-cream outlets, a snake park, Seaworld and the Dolphinarium (► 52).

Ice World
Ice rink with skates for hire. Ice skating shows held here from time to time, consult local press for details.
☒ **Sol Harris Crescent**
☎ **031-332 4597**

Mitchell Park
Parents can sit under the lovely old trees while the children play on the swings, run around on the lawns, or look at the birds and guinea pigs in cages. A restaurant offers teas and light meals.
☒ **Innes Road, Morningside**

The Wheel
Many amusements for children at this large mall (► 108).

KwaZulu-Natal, South Coast
Many of the resorts here are geared for family holidays. Children will enjoy a train trip on the Banana Express and the shells at the Shell Museum (► 57).

Margate Pleasureland
Fun fair with dodgem cars, big Wheel, water slide and a variety of rides for children.
☒ **Margate Beach** ☎ **(cell) 039-312 0864**

KwaZulu-Natal, North Coast
Teenagers might like to see sharks being dissected; most will enjoy the reptiles at Tongaat's Crocodile Creek (► 57).

Johannesburg
Gold Reef City
Theme park with many rides

and amusements for children(► 67).

Johannesburg Zoo and Zoo Lake
One of the best places in this city to take the family: bears, lions, elephants, and rowing-boats on the lake (► 70).

Newtown Cultural Precinct
The Afrika Cultural Centre here, located in a converted warehouse, has a Creative Workshop for youngsters, as well as a resource centre and children's museum (► 70).
☎ **011-838 4541**

Planetarium
Runs Saturday morning shows designed specially for children aged 5 to 8.
☒ **Yale Road** ☎ **011-717 1392;**
www.wits.ac.za/planetarium
🕒 **Sat 10:30**

Randburg Waterfront
Has large children's entertainment centre, complete with ten-pin bowling, laser-quest games, video games and a carousel for younger children (► 71).

Pretoria
Children will enjoy the outstanding zoo and its cable-cars (► 75) and the stuffed birds, with recorded birdsong, at the Transvaal Museum (► 75).

Sun City
This complex employs full-time organisers of children's entertainment, and has water activities at the Valley of the Waves and a petting zoo (► 87).

Safety
Although the locals are very child-friendly, safety-consciousness is not highly developed in South Africa, so you will need to keep a close eye on your children while touring. Only at some major tourist beaches and swimming pools will you find lifeguards on duty. Many monuments and lookout points have no safety barriers, or at best only minimal ones, to guard against a potential fall.

Nightclubs & Live Music/Theatres

Music Mix
With its mix of cultural styles, South Africa has a rich tradition of musical performance. Styles include the township sounds of kwaito, mainstream and African jazz, African-Western fusion, Western classical music, indigenous traditional drumming, minstrel banjo-strumming and alternative Afrikaans rock. You don't have to go to a club or theatre to hear live music: talented buskers of all kinds perform in public during the summer.

Opening Times
Clubs and live music venues are generally open from 8PM until early morning.

Nightclubs & Live Music

Cape Town

Kennedy's
Up-market venue offering live jazz, a smoking room with an international selection of cigars, and a restaurant with an eclectic menu and a fine wine list.
✉ 251 Long Street ☎ 021-424 1212; e-mail: kennedys@netactive.co.za ⊕ Mon–Sat, until late

The Green Dolphin
Fairly pricey restaurant, but pleasing venue; one of the best live jazz locales in the city.
✉ Pierhead, Victoria and Alfred Waterfront ☎ 021-421 7471 ⊕ Daily

Rhodes House
Expensive, but internationally highly rated nightclub housed in an historic monument. Offers R&B, hip-hop, and themed evenings.
✉ 60 Queen Victoria Street ☎ 021-424 8844; e-mail: info@rhodeshouse.com ⊕ Dec–Apr Mon–Sat; May–Nov Thu and Sat

Durban

Club 330
This is a highly rated, late-night dance club where leading DJs play house, techno and trance.
✉ 330 Point Road ☎ 031-337 7172 ⊕ Sat night only

Angelo's Cantina
Smooth R&B is on the music menu at this popular dance club and cocktail bar in the city centre.
✉ 24 West Street ☎ 031-332 3967 ⊕ Closed Tue and Sun

Bat Centre
Art development and community centre overlooking the harbour. Has a restaurant, a bar and a large auditorium, all offering regular performances of live music.
✉ 45 Maritime Place, Small Craft Harbour ☎ 031-332 0451

Rainbow Restaurant and Jazz Club
One of the oldest live jazz locales in the province. Phone for details of performances.
✉ Shop 6, 23 Stanford Lane, Pinetown ☎ 031-702 9161

Thirsty's
Nicely situated overlooking the harbour mouth, this bar/restaurant features funk and jazz groups right through the week.
✉ Point Waterfront ☎ 031-337 9212 ⊕ Daily 8AM–midnight

Johannesburg

Gramadoelas (► 97)
This restaurant features a wide range of live African music.
✉ Market Theatre Complex ☎ 011-838 6960

Kippies Jazz International
One of the country's leading jazz bars, showcasing jazz and fusion by top local and international musicians.
✉ Corner of Bree and Wolhuter (Market Theatre Complex, ► 70) ☎ 011-833 3316 ⊕ Daily 10PM till late

Roxy Rhythm Bar
Live music spot offering original acts almost every night of the week; occasional DJs.
✉ Corner of Main Road and 5th

Avenue, Melville ☎ 011-726 6019 🕐 Daily

Pretoria

Café Barcelona
Live bands play their blues, jazz and rock compositions at this restaurant/bar.
✉ Elardus Park Shopping Centre, Barnard Street ☎ 021-345 3602 🕐 Mon–Sat noon–2AM

Firkin Pub
Wide variety of live bands and styles of music on offer.
✉ Corner of Hendrik Verwoerd and Embankment roads
☎ 012-663 4213
🕐 Mon–Sat noon–2AM

Theatres
Consult the local press for details of performances.

Cape Town

Artscape Theatre Complex
Large complex with several performance areas, featuring dance, plays, musicals, concerts and opera.
✉ D F Malan Street ☎ 021-410 9919

Baxter Theatre Centre
Variety of theatres offering all types of performing arts.
✉ Rondebosch ☎ 021-685 7880

Theatre On The Bay
Smallish theatre offering good-quality commercial plays and farces.
✉ 1 Link Street, Camps Bay
☎ 021-438 3301

Durban

Durban Playhouse Theatre Complex
The complex includes a graceful opera house, and a variety of other venues, providing a complete range of performing arts.
✉ 29 Acutt Street ☎ 031-369 9555

Elizabeth Sneddon Theatre
Large multi-purpose auditorium, used for a variety of performances. Annual film festival held in October.
✉ University of Natal, King George V Avenue ☎ 031-260 2296

Johannesburg

Barnyard Theatre
Unusual dinner and live music theatre venue, where you bring your own food or order in pizza
✉ Broadacre Centre, Cedar and Valley roads, Four Ways
☎ 011-467 9333 🕐 Mon–Sat evenings

Johannesburg Civic Theatre
The five performance spaces here are used for music, opera, dance and theatre.
✉ Simmonds Street, Braamfontein ☎ 011-877 6800; www.artslink.co.ze/civic

Market Theatre Foundation
(➤ 70)

Pretoria

State Theatre
One of the top venues in the country, offering all genres of the performing arts, including symphony concerts and opera.
✉ 320 Pretorius Street
☎ 012-392 4000

Bloemfontein

Bloemfontein Civic Theatre
The auditorium seats 450 and is used primarily for drama productions.
✉ Markgraf Street ☎ 051-447 7771

Drama Today
Under apartheid, politically engaged protest theatre flourished locally while the best international artists boycotted the country. Nowadays good theatre from all over the world is again available, and local playwrights are beginning to explore the new feelings of optimism and anxiety abroad in South Africa. Forms such as comedies and musicals, which might have been thought frivolous a decade or two ago, are once more becoming popular.

Sport

Sports in South Africa
South Africa's warm climate makes it an ideal place for outdoor activities. Just about all the major team and individual sports are practised here, apart from winter sports. Many sports clubs welcome visitors who would like to play tennis or a round of golf, or to go diving, boating or waterskiing. Simply enquire at your hotel or guest house, make a phone call and ask what facilities are available.

Spectator Sports
South African sports with the largest following are soccer, rugby and cricket. The following stadiums host major local and international matches during the appropriate season:

Newlands Cricket Ground, Cape Town
Wonderfully scenic venue; cricket in summer and some soccer in winter.
✉ Campground Road, Newlands ☎ 021-657 2003

Newlands Rugby Ground, Cape Town
Rugby and some soccer in winter.
✉ Boundary Road, Newlands
☎ 021-659 4500

King's Park, Durban
Rugby and soccer in winter.
✉ Jacko Jackson Drive
☎ 031-308 8400

Wanderers, Johannesburg
Cricket in summer.
✉ Corlett Drive, Illovo ☎ 011-788 1008

Ellis Park, Johannesburg
Rugby and soccer in winter.
✉ Corner of Curry and Staib roads, Doornfontein ☎ 011-402 8644

Loftus Versveld, Pretoria
Rugby in winter.
✉ Kirkness Street, Arcadia
☎ 012-344 4011

Participant Sports

Ballooning
Flights are offered in the high interior of the country where weather conditions are most stable.
Bill Harrop's 'Original' Balloon Safaris
☎ 011-705 3201;
www.balloon.co.za

Canoeing & Rafting
South Africa offers the full range of conditions, from adrenalin-pumping white-water trips, to a gentle drift downstream. Single- and multi-day excursions available.
Felix Unite Tourism Group
✉ 141 Landsdowne Road, Claremont ☎ 021-670 1300;
www.felixunite.com

Cycling & Mountain Biking
Cycling is not advised in or around the cities or on major roads, as local drivers are not cyclist-friendly. But scenic mountain biking trails can be found countrywide.
Wild Thing Tours
✉ Long Street, Cape Town
☎ 021-423 5804;
www.wildthing.co.za

Cape Argus Cycle Tour
The annual Cape Argus Cycle Tour is the biggest event of its kind in the world and attracts 30,000 participants of all levels of skill. The tour covers 105km through the Cape Peninsula.
☎ 021-905 6551;
www.cycletour.co.za

Fishing
You can do fly-fishing in the rivers of the Western Cape, Drakensberg and Mpumalanga, and game-fishing from most coastal resorts along the southwestern and eastern seaboards of South Africa.
Piscatorial Society
☎ 021-424 7725
Sport Fishing Information
☎ 021-447 6010

Golf

There are many golf courses around the country, in the large cities and in major holiday areas, such as the Garden Route, the KwaZulu-Natal South Coast and Mpumalanga. Most welcome visitors. Several cities have municipal courses, open to all.

Gyms

All large centres, as well as many of the up-market hotels, have gyms and fitness centres where visitors are welcome. Virgin Active has many branches countrywide.

Cape Region
☎ 021-710 8750

Gauteng North
☎ 012-665 4490

Guateng South
☎ 011-884 4492

Natal Region
☎ 031-572 3757

Hiking

The best areas for hiking are the Western Cape, the Garden Route, Drakensberg and Mpumalanga. The country has a large number of multi-day hiking-trails with overnight huts which can be booked through the National Parks Board.

National Parks Board
☎ 012-428 9111

Table Mountain Walks
A variety of routes exploring this famous landmark.
✉ 8 Le Parc, Park Avenue, Tokai, Cape Town ☎ 021-715 6136 (and fax); e-mail: mcurran@mweb.co.za; www.tablemountainwalks.co.za

Horse Riding

Many single- or multi-day riding trails (the best areas are the same as for Hiking).

Jacana Country Homes and Trails
✉ 291 Aurigu Street, Waterkloof Ridge, Pretoria
☎ 012-346 3550;
www.jacanacollection.co.za

Running

Road-running is a well-established sport throughout South Africa. The following two long-distance races draw tens of thousands of participants each year, from South Africa and abroad.

Two Oceans Marathon
The 56km annual marathon takes place on Easter Saturday, through the superbly scenic Cape Peninsula. It normally draws a field of 15,000.
✉ Two Oceans Marathon Office, PO Box 2276, Clareinch 77401231 ☎ 021-671 9407 www.twooceansmarathon.org.za

Comrades Marathon
This 90km race, from Pietermaritzburg to Durban (vice versa in alternate years) takes place mid-June, drawing a field of over 20,000 participants.
✉ Comrades Marathon Association, 18 Connaught Road, Scottsville 3209 ☎ 033-394 3510; www.comrades.org.za

Watersports

Diving instruction, waterskiing and sea-kayaking are available at many coastal resorts and also on some large inland rivers and dams.

Pulse Africa Tour Operators
☎ 011-327 0468;
www.africansafari.co.za

A Sports-mad Nation

If you talk to the locals you will soon discover that they are passionate about their sport. Ask blacks which soccer team they support – the Chiefs (Kaiser Chiefs), the Buccaneers (Orlando Pirates) or the Birds (Moroka Swallows) – or how Bafana Bafana (the Boys, nickname for the national team) are doing. A good all-purpose question for whites is, 'What do you think of the Bokke?' (Springboks, now the name only for the national rugby team, but still widely used of any national team.)

What's On When

A Feast of Festivals

Many smaller towns around the country have cottoned on to the fact that festivals attract visitors – both local and international. The pioneers were Grahamstown with its arts festival – now the world's biggest, after Edinburgh – and Ficksburg, with its long-established annual Cherry Festival (► 89). Now there are festivals of poetry, film, arts, dance and theatre, not to mention whales, wine, brandy and even cheese. Look in the local newspapers for details.

January

A different Shakespeare play is produced each year in the beautiful outdoor setting of *Maynardville Park*, Wynberg, Cape Town.
☎ 021-421 5470

March

Farmers from all over the region bring their antique machines to the unique *Vintage Tractor Show* held during the first week of March at Sandstone Estate, Flicksburg in the Free State.
☎ 051-933 2619

April

Johannesburg's *Rand Easter Show*, held annually for ten days around Easter, is a huge mix of trade exhibitions and demonstrations, speciality events and funfairs.
☎ 011-661 4000

May

Poetry Africa in Durban is an annual celebration of poetry, with participants from many countries.
☎ 031-260 2506

June–July

From the last week in June, for ten days, Grahamstown comes alive with the *National Arts Festival* – by far Southern Africa's biggest. Features are music, dance, drama and visual arts from Africa and the rest of the world. Many other events and huge craft markets take over the streets.
☎ 046-603 1100

August

Oppikoppi Music Festival, one of the country's biggest, features up to 80 local rock bands performing in the bushveld, about two hours from Johannesburg.
☎ 083-258 2595

September

Arts Alive in Johannesburg showcases local and international music, dance and theatre.
☎ 011-786 8514

The *Knysna Arts Festival* is a feast of visual, performing and community arts, with jazz, cabaret and classical concerts.
☎ 044-382 5510

North West Cultural Calabash in the remote village of Taung has become a major annual showcase for African performing arts.
☎ 053-994 2404

October

The arrival of the whales is celebrated at the *Hermanus Whale Festival* by live music, a craft market, and arts and environmental activities.
☎ 082-775 8843

November

From November until the end of March, Cape Town's *Spier Festival* offers music, opera and drama in an open-air theatre on the beautiful Spier Wine Estate.
☎ 021-809 1100

When its thousands of cherry trees are in bloom, late in November, Ficksburg in the Free State celebrates the *Cherry Festival*.
☎ 051-933 4872

December

The *Oude Libertas Summer Festival* in Stellenbosch begins in December and runs till March, offering drama, dance, opera and music in a graceful open-air auditorium.
☎ 021-809 7473

Practical Matters

Above: a wigwam of
surfboards on Durban beach
Right: a multi-lingual sign on
one of South Africa's beaches

GMT 12 noon	South Africa 2PM	Germany 1PM	USA (NY) 7AM	Netherlands 1PM	Spain 1PM

BEFORE YOU GO

WHAT YOU NEED

		UK	Germany	USA	Netherlands	Spain
● Required ○ Suggested ▲ Not required	Some countries require a passport to remain valid for a minimum period (usually at least six months) beyond the date of entry – contact their consulate or embassy or your travel agent for details.					
Passport		●	●	●	●	●
Visa (regulations can change – check before booking your journey)		▲	●	▲	●	●
Onward or return ticket		●	●	●	●	●
Health inoculations		○	○	○	○	○
Health documentation (► 123, Health)		▲	▲	▲	▲	▲
Travel insurance		●	●	●	●	●
Driving licence (national)		●	●	●	●	●
Car insurance certificate		●	●	●	●	●
Car registration document		●	●	●	●	●

WHEN TO GO

Cape Town

High season

Low season

21°C	21°C	20°C	18°C	15°C	13°C	12°C	13°C	14°C	16°C	18°C	20°C
JAN	FEB	MAR	APR	MAY	JUN	JUL	AUG	SEP	OCT	NOV	DEC
☀	☀	☀	☀	⛅	🌧	🌧	🌧	⛅	⛅	⛅	☀

☀ Sun   ⛅ Sun/showers   🌧 Wet

TOURIST OFFICES

In the UK
South African Tourism
No. 5 and 6 Alt Grove
Wimbledon
London SW19 4DZ
☎ 020 8971 9352
info@uk.southafrica.net

In the USA
South African Tourism
500 Fifth Avenue
20th Floor
Suite 2040
New York NY 10110
☎ 212 730 2929
newyork@southafrica.net

www.south-african-tourism.org

POLICE (FLYING SQUAD) 10111

FIRE 1022 (ASK FOR FIRE)

AMBULANCE 10177 (ASK FOR AMBULANCE)

WHEN YOU ARE THERE

ARRIVING

Most visitors arrive at Johannesburg and Cape Town international airports. South Africa has borders with six other southern African countries; border posts are open 8–6 daily. There are rail links with Namibia, Zimbabwe, Botswana and Mozambique.

Johannesburg Airport
Distance to city centre

25 kilometres

Journey times	
🚇	N/A
🚌	35 minutes
🚗	35 minutes

Cape Town Airport
Distance to city centre

22 kilometres

Journey times	
🚇	N/A
🚌	20 minutes
🚗	20 minutes

MONEY

The monetary unit is the Rand, divided into 100 cents. R10, R20, R50, R100 and R200 notes are available. Major credit cards are widely accepted in all major centres. Most banks have exchange control facilities but will require identification. MasterCard holders may use any Thomas Cook network location to report loss or theft, and to obtain an emergency card free of charge.

TIME

🕐 **L** South African Standard Time is 2 hours ahead of Greenwich Mean Time (GMT+2), so only one hour ahead of Britain during British summer time. The whole country lies within the same time zone. But the Western Cape, lying furthest to the south and west, has long summer evenings.

CUSTOMS

→ **YES**

Visitors over 18 are entitled to the following allowances:
Cigarettes: 400
Cigars: 50
Cigarette or pipe tobacco: 250 grams
Wine: 2 litres
Spirits or other alcoholic beverages: 1 litre
Perfume: 50ml
Toilet water: 250ml
Gifts, souvenirs and other goods up to a value of R1250,00
Flat rate assessment:
You may elect to pay duty at a flat rate of 20 per cent on goods up to a value of R10 000,00 over and above your duty-free allowance.

— **NO**

Drugs are prohibited. If you are carrying prescription medication, bring a letter from your doctor.

UK	Germany	Netherlands	Spain	US
011-537 7206	012-427 8999	012-344 3910	021-422 2415	012-342 1048

WHEN YOU ARE THERE

TOURIST OFFICES

Western Cape Tourism Board
- Pinnacle Building
Corner of Berg and Castle streets
Cape Town 8000
☎ 021 426-5639

Cape Town Tourism
- 3 Adderley Street
Cape Town
☎ 021-426 4260

Durban Africa
- 160 Pine Street
2nd Floor Station Building
Durban
☎ 031-304 4934

North West Province Tourism
☎ 012-386 1225

Pretoria Tourism
- Head Office
442 Rigel Avenue
South Erasmusrand 0181
☎ 012-310 3911

SA Tourism and Tourism Johannesburg
- 12 Rivonia Road, Illovo,
Johannesburg
☎ 011-778 8000

NATIONAL HOLIDAYS

J	F	M	A	M	J	J	A	S	O	N	D
1		1(2)	2(2)	1	1		1	1			3

1 January	New Year's Day
22 March	Human Rights Day
March/April	Good Friday
March/April	Family Day
22 April	Freedom Day
1 May	Workers Day
16 June	Youth Day
9 August	National Women's Day
24 September	Heritage Day
16 December	Day of Reconciliation
25 December	Christmas Day
26 December	Day of Goodwill

Public holidays apply to all workers.
School holidays: mid-December to late January (6 weeks); Easter (4 weeks); July–August (5 weeks).

OPENING HOURS

○ Shops	● Attractions/museums
● Offices	● Churches, mosques etc
● Banks	● Pharmacies

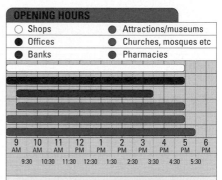

9 AM	10 AM	11 AM	12 PM	1 PM	2 PM	3 PM	4 PM	5 PM	6 PM
9:30	10:30	11:30	12:30	1:30	2:30	3:30	4:30	5:30	

In many small towns shops do not open on Sunday and it is wise to stock up on food and other essentials on Saturday. Banks are also open on Saturday morning 9–11. Museum opening times vary; check individual listings. All major centres have pharmacies which are open 24 hours – check in the telephone book. Many churches, mosques and synagogues are open 7–5 seven days a week, but check locally.

DRIVE ON THE LEFT

TOILETS GOOD

Toilets are sometimes primitive in nature reserves and parks but are usually very clean.

PUBLIC TRANSPORT

Internal flights
There Is an excellent domestic network serving all the cities, some of the main tourist sights, such as Kruger NP, and a surprising number of the smaller towns. Fares are not particularly cheap but pre-booking will ensure discounts.

Trains
Most of the major centres are linked by rail, but because of the terrain, these links are often very circuitous. First-class is cheap, safe, comfortable and spacious. The trains are slow by European standards but offer linen sheets and blankets and old-fashioned meals in a dining car. The luxury Blue Train runs between Cape Town and Pretoria. Short trips by steam train are available in several centres.

Buses
Long-distance coaches offer a popular form of travel and all inter-city routes are serviced. It is necessary to book in advance. The three main operators are Greyhound Citiliner, Intercape and the Translux Express.

Urban Transport
Very little public transport is suitable for tourists in the cities, except for the suburban railway in Cape Town and the Mynah shuttle in Durban.

CAR RENTAL

Car rental firms have offices throughout the country and offer good service. Local firms offer a cheaper rate but a more limited service. Car rental is expensive and it is advisable to shop around for deals. With the huge distances to be covered check for unlimited mileage offers. Ensure you have a full set of tools and spares before setting out.

TAXIS

There is a growing armada of minibus 'taxis' on the roads. Though inexpensive they are noisy and often overloaded, and are not recommended for visitors except on familiar main routes. Regular taxis are metered and expensive. They can be summoned by phone or caught at a rank but may not be hailed in the street.

DRIVING

Speed limit on freeways: **120kph**

Speed limit on rural roads: **100kph**

Speed limit in built-up areas: **60kph**

Compulsory both for drivers and passengers at all times.

There is random breathalyser testing for drivers, primarily in the urban areas. Drunken driving is severely punished.

Leaded and unleaded petrol and diesel are available everywhere in South Africa. Fuel is relatively cheap. Credit cards are not accepted.

The British AA/RAC has reciprocal arrangements with other national driving associations and will give advice and travel information as well as arrange emergency breakdown services. Be wary of predatory breakdown trucks, whose operators sometimes charge exorbitant rates.

PERSONAL SAFETY

Most South African cities have a security problem. Central Cape Town and Durban require normal vigilance during daylight hours but parts of Johannesburg are virtual no-go areas. The first rule is to try not to look affluent. Don't walk the streets festooned with cameras and jewellery; if you must carry valuables, put them in an old shopping bag. Use credit cards and travellers' cheques where possible and avoid carrying large amounts of cash. Do not walk alone after dark, take a taxi instead. If you are mugged, hand over your valuables and do not resist. Wait till your assailant is out of sight and then call the police. Keep car windows and doors locked and do not pick up hitchhikers or stop to help people; phone the police instead. Always park in well lit and preferably busy places.

Police assistance:
☎ 10111 from any call box

TELEPHONES

The telephone service is good and many public phones have been installed recently. Phonecards for the green public call boxes are available in most cafés and pubs.

The international dialing code for South Africa is 27. International direct dial is 09 followed by the country code

International Dialling Codes

From South Africa to:

UK:	44
Germany:	49
Canada:	1
USA:	1
Netherlands:	599

POST

South Africa has a good and relatively inexpensive postal service, which is available during regular business hours. All post offices have public phones attached and phone cards are available. Poste restante services are available in the main post office in each town. Remember to take identification in order to claim mail.

ELECTRICITY

220–230 volts AC 50Hz. Sockets take three round pins. Adaptors for square

pins are available but may be in short supply. Power is reliable in towns, but may be intermittent in remote areas, where it is advisable to bring a torch. US appliances may need a transformer.

TIPS/GRATUITIES

Yes ✓ No ✗		
Restaurants	✓	10–15%
Bar service	✗	
Taxis	✓	R5
Tour guides (per day)	✓	R20–R30
Hairdressers	✓	R5
Chambermaids	✓	R5–R10
Porters (per item)	✓	R2
Hairdressers	✓	R1–2
Theatre/cinema attendants	✗	
Toilets	✗	

What to photograph: there are no restrictions on photographing buildings; ask permission if you wish to photograph a person.
When to photograph: the local light is generally strong, make adjustments to avoid overexposure. Early morning and late evening light are best for scenic and animal photography. Take a telephoto lens.
Where to buy film: film is available in all supermarkets, pharmacies and most cafés.

HEALTH

Medical Treatment In larger centres, the medical and hospital services are excellent. Doctors are listed in the telephone directory under Medical Practitioners. All hospitals have a 24-hour emergency service and most family doctors have a designated after hours practitioner. The number will be on the answer machine of the regular practice.

Aids is endemic, with some 15 per cent of the sexually active population estimated to be HIV positive. Practise celibacy or safe sex. Condoms are freely available. Blood for medicinal purposes is carefully screened and treated.

Dental Services Dentists are listed in the telephone book under Medical Practioners. There is usually an number on the answer machine for emergencies that occur after hours.

Sun Advice Wear a hat, high-factor sun block and stay in the shade in the intense midday heat. Remember to keep up your liquid intake. If you become dehydrated, take a cool bath and drink plenty of water.

Drugs All cities and main towns have pharmacies and dispensing pharmacists who will advise you on appropriate medication. Malaria is endemic in the northern and northeastern parts of the country. You must start using the appropriate medication a week before you plan to visit a malaria area and continue for 4–5 weeks after you have left.

Safe Water Tap water is safe. In bush camps check before drinking. Purify water from rivers and lakes (boiling/purification tablets). Mineral water is freely available. Do not swim or paddle without checking to see if bilharzia, crocodile or hippo are present.

CONCESSIONS

Student/Youths Most airlines, rail and coach travel have concessions for youths and students. Student concessions are available in museums, art galleries and some tourist venues on request. Be prepared to produce valid identification.

Senior citizens Discounts are available on rail, coaches and some airlines. Discounted entrance tariffs for senior citizens are available in most museums and tourist venues. Be prepared to ask and produce a document to validate your status.

CLOTHING SIZES

South Africa	UK	Rest of Europe	USA	
92	36	46	36	Suits
497	38	48	38	Suits
102	40	50	40	Suits
107	42	52	42	Suits
112	44	54	44	Suits
117	46	56	46	Suits
7	7	41	8	Shoes
7.5	7.5	42	8.5	Shoes
8.5	8.5	43	9.5	Shoes
9	9.5	44	10.5	Shoes
10	10.5	45	11.5	Shoes
11	11	46	12	Shoes
14.5	14.5	37	14.5	Shirts
15	15	38	15	Shirts
15.5	15.5	39/40	15.5	Shirts
16	16	41	16	Shirts
16.5	16.5	42	16.5	Shirts
17	17	43	17	Shirts
82	8	34	6	Dresses
87	10	36	8	Dresses
92	12	38	10	Dresses
97	14	40	12	Dresses
102	16	42	14	Dresses
107	18	44	16	Dresses
5	4.5	38	6	Shoes
5.5	5	38	6.5	Shoes
6	5.5	39	7	Shoes
6.5	6	39	7.5	Shoes
7	6.5	40	8	Shoes
7.5	7	41	8.5	Shoes

WHEN DEPARTING

- Check that any airport or other taxes are included in the price of your ticket.
- Reconfirm all flights at least 72 hours before the time of departure.
- Ensure that you arrive at the airport two hours before the time of departure, making allowance for traffic jams at rush hour.

LANGUAGE

South Africa has 11 official languages, but in the cities you will need only English. In rural areas and small towns all over the country Afrikaans is widely used. Although for practical purposes you are unlikely to need to use the African languages, you will meet with a very friendly response if you attempt some of the basic words and phrases listed below. Xhosa is spoken in the Western and Eastern Cape, and understood in KwaZulu-Natal; Sotho is spoken in the Free State, Gauteng and much of the Northern Province.

English	Afrikaans	English	Africaans
hotel	hotel	room service	kamerbedi-ening
bed and breakfast	bed en ontbyt	chambermaid	kamerdiens
single room	enkelkamer	bath	bad
double room	dubbelkamer	shower	stortbad
one person	een persoon	toilet	toilet
one night	een nag	balcony	balkon
reservation	bespreking	key	sleutel
bank	bank	travellers' cheque	reisigerstjek
exchange office	geld-wisselkantoor	credit card	kredietkaart
post office	poskantoor	exchange rate	wisselkoors
coin	muntstuk	commission charge	kommissie
banknote	banknoot		
cheque	tjek	cashier	kassie
pub/bar	kroeg	starter	voorgereg
restaurant	restourant	main course	hoofgereg
breakfast	ontbyt	dessert	nagereg
lunch	middagete	bill	rekening
dinner	aandete	beer	bier
table	tafel	wine	wyn
waiter	kelner	milk	melk
waitress	kelnerin	coffee	koffie
aeroplane	vliegtuig	single ticket	enkelkaartjie
airport	lughawe	return ticket	retour-kaartjie
train	trein	non-smoking	nie-roker
bus	bus	car	motor
station	stasie	petrol	brandstoff
boat	boot	bus stop	bushalte
port	hawe	how do I get to...?	hoe kom ek by...?
ticket	kaartjie		

Useful phrases English	Afrikaans	Sotho	Xhosa
yes	ja	ewe	e
no	nee	hayi	tjhe
please	asseblief	nceda	hle
thank you	dankie	enkosi	ke a leboha
hello	hallo	molo	helele
how are you?	hoe gaan dit?	ujani?	o a phila?
goodbye	tot siens	sala kahle	gabotse

Acknowledgements

The Automobile would like to thank the following photographers, libraries and associations for the their assistance in the preparation of this book.

ART DIRECTORS AND TRIP PHOTO LIBRARY 25b, 36b, 39, 89b; MARY EVANS PICTURE LIBRARY 10b, 11, 31b; J HOWARD 17C; HUMAN AND ROUSSEAU (PTY) LTD 78b; PICTURES COLOUR LIBRARY 20b, 46b, 52, 74, 76b, 76c, 79c, 88a; REX FEATURES LTD 14b, 14c; SPECTRUM COLOUR LIBRARY 13c, 24b, 47, 50b, 63b, 63c; WORLD PICTURES 18c, 25c, 57

The remaining pictures are held in the Association's own library (AA PHOTOLIBRARY) and were taken by CLIVE SAWYER with the exception of the following:
M BIRKITT 15a, 16a, 17a, 18a, 19a, 20a, 21a, 22a, 24a, 25a, 26a, 49, 53a, 54, 55a, 58a, 60a, 61a, 62a, 63a, 66b, 70b; CARRIE HAMPTON 1, 9b, 22b, 23c, 58b, 90b, 91a, 92, 93, 94, 95, 96, 97, 98, 99, 100, 101, 102, 103, 104, 105, 106, 107, 108, 109, 110, 111, 112, 113, 114, 115, 116; PAUL KENWARD 5b, 6c, 7c, 8b, 12b, 12c, 17b, 18b, 31c, 36c, 42a, 42b, 43b, 44b, 46a, 48, 50a, 50c, 56b, 59b, 59c, 65, 68, 69, 70c, 71b, 73a, 75b, 76a, 78c, 79a, 84b, 117a; RICHARD WHITAKER 59a, 122a, 122b

Author's Acknowledgements

Richard Whitaker would like to thank the staff of the Cape Town Tourism Board for their help, and his wife, Jennie, for all her logistical and emotional support.

Revision management: Pam Stagg Page layout: Tony Truscott

Dear Essential Traveller

Your comments, opinions and recommendations are very important to us. So please help us to improve our travel guides by taking a few minutes to complete this simple questionnaire.

You do not need a stamp (unless posted outside the UK). If you do not want to cut this page from your guide, then photocopy it or write your answers on a plain sheet of paper.

Send to: **The Editor, AA World Travel Guides, FREEPOST SCE 4598, Basingstoke RG21 4GY.**

Your recommendations...

We always encourage readers' recommendations for restaurants, nightlife or shopping – if your recommendation is used in the next edition of the guide, we will send you a *FREE* AA *Essential* **Guide** of your choice. Please state below the establishment name, location and your reasons for recommending it.

_____

_____

_____

_____

Please send me **AA *Essential*** _____

About this guide...

Which title did you buy?
AA *Essential* _____
Where did you buy it? _____
When? m m / y y

Why did you choose an AA *Essential* Guide? _____

_____

_____

_____

_____

Did this guide meet your expectations?
Exceeded ☐   Met all ☐   Met most ☐   Fell below ☐
Please give your reasons _____

_____

_____

_____

continued on next page...

Were there any aspects of this guide that you particularly liked? _____

_____

_____

Is there anything we could have done better? _____

_____

_____

About you...

Name (*Mr/Mrs/Ms*) _____

Address _____

_____

_____ Postcode _____

Daytime tel nos _____

Please only give us your mobile phone number if you wish to hear from us
about other products and services from the AA and partners by text or mms.

Which age group are you in?
Under 25 ☐   25–34 ☐   35–44 ☐   45–54 ☐   55–64 ☐   65+ ☐

How many trips do you make a year?
Less than one ☐   One ☐   Two ☐   Three or more ☐

Are you an AA member? Yes ☐   No ☐

About your trip...

When did you book? m m / y y   When did you travel? m m / y y

How long did you stay? _____

Was it for business or leisure? _____

Did you buy any other travel guides for your trip?

If yes, which ones? _____

Thank you for taking the time to complete this questionnaire. Please send it to us as soon as
possible, and remember, you do not need a stamp (*unless posted outside the UK*).

Happy Holidays!

The information we hold about you will be used to provide the products and services requested
and for identification, account administration, analysis, and fraud/loss prevention purposes. More
details about how that information is used is in our privacy statement, which you'll find under the
heading "Personal Information" in our terms and conditions and on our website: www.theAA.com.
Copies are also available from us by post, by contacting the Data Protection Manager at AA,
Southwood East, Apollo Rise, Farnborough, Hampshire GU14 0JW.

We may want to contact you about other products and services provided by us, or our partners (by
mail, telephone) but please tick the box if you DO NOT wish to hear about such products and
services from us by mail or telephone. ☐

The Atlas

Acknowledgements
All pictures are from AA World Travel Library with contributions from the following photographer:
Paul Kenward : Cape Town harbour, flowers in meadow, Gold Reef City, Diani Beach near Mombasa

The Automobile Association
www.theAA.com
The Automobile Association's website offers comprehensive and up-to-the-minute information covering AA-approved hotels, guest houses and B&Bs, restaurants and pubs in the UK; airport parking, insurance, European breakdown cover, European motoring advice, a ferry planner, European route planner, overseas fuel prices, a bookshop and much more.

The Foreign and Commonwealth Office
Country advice, traveller's tips, before you
go information, checklists and more.
www.fco.gov.uk

Official South African Tourism Website
www.south-african-tourism.org

GENERAL
UK Passport Service
www.ukpa.gov.uk

Health Advice for Travellers
www.doh.gov.uk/traveladvice

UK Travel Insurance Directory
www.uktravelinsurancedirectory.co.uk

BBC – Holiday
www.bbc.co.uk/holiday

The Full Universal Currency Converter
www.xe.com/ucc/full.shtml

Flying with Kids
www.flyingwithkids.com

www.capeinfosa.co.za
www.durban.org.za
www.kzn.org.za
www.drakensberg.kzn.org.za/drakensberg
www.going2africa.com
www.krugerpark.co.za
www.ecoafrica.com
www.parks-sa.co.za

TRAVEL
Flights and Information
www.cheapflights.co.uk
www.thisistravel.co.uk
www.ba.com
www.worldairportguide.com

Highway, multilane divided road - under construction Autobahn, mehrspurige Straße - in Bau		Autoroute, route à plusieurs voies - en construction Autosnelweg, weg met meer rijstroken - in aanleg
Trunk road - under construction Fernverkehrsstraße - in Bau		Route à grande circulation - en construction Weg voor interlokaal verkeer - in aanleg
Principal highway Hauptstraße		Route principale Hoofdweg
Secondary road Nebenstraße		Route secondaire Overige verharde wegen
Practicable road, track Fahrweg, Piste		Chemin carrossable, piste Weg, piste
Road numbering Straßennummerierung	C 33 B 2 R 521 N 1	Numérotage des routes Wegnummering
Distances in kilometres Entfernungen in Kilometer	130 **259** 129	Distances en kilomètres Afstand in kilometers
Height in metres - Pass Höhe in Meter - Pass	136 •	Altitude en mètres - Col Hoogte in meters - Pas
Railway - Railway ferry Eisenbahn - Eisenbahnfähre		Chemin de fer - Ferry-boat Spoorweg - Spoorpont
Car ferry - Shipping route Autofähre - Schifffahrtslinie		Bac autos - Ligne maritime Autoveer - Scheepvaartlijn
Major international airport - Airport Wichtiger internationaler Flughafen - Flughafen	✈	Aéroport importante international - Aéroport Belangrijke internationale luchthaven - Luchthaven
International boundary - Province boundary Internationale Grenze - Provinzgrenze		Frontière internationale - Limite de Province Internationale grens - Provinciale grens
Undefined boundary Unbestimmte Grenze		Frontière d'Etat non définie Rijksgrens onbepaalt
National capital Hauptstadt eines souveränen Staates	**BOGOTÁ**	Capitale nationale Hoofdstad van een souvereine staat
Federal capital Hauptstadt eines Bundesstaates	**Boa Vista**	Capitale d'un état fédéral Hoofdstad van een deelstat
National park Nationalpark		Parc national Nationaal park
Ancient monument Antikes Baudenkmal	∴	Localité remarquable Bezienswaardige plaats
Interesting cultural monument Sehenswertes Kulturdenkmal	* Rock Paintings	Monument culturel intéressant Bezienswaardig cultuurmonument
Interesting natural monument Sehenswertes Naturdenkmal	* Sudwala Caves	Monuments naturel intéressant Bezienswaardig natuurmonument
Well Brunnen	⌣	Puits Bron

134-141	0 ————————— 100 km 0 ————————— 50 miles	
142-143	0 ————————— 500 m 0 ————————— 500 yards	

Maps © Mairs Geographischer Verlag / Falk Verlag, 73751 Ostfildern

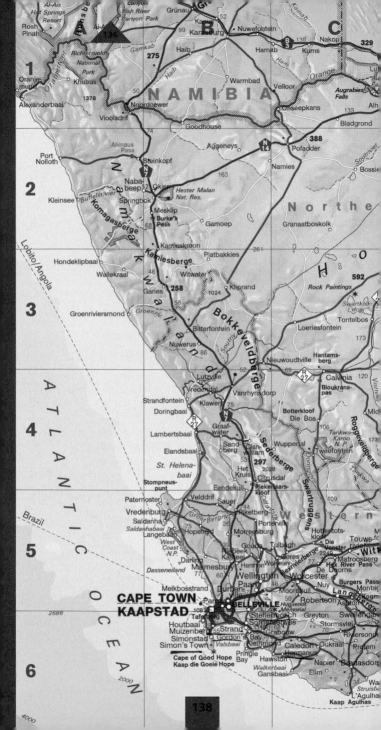

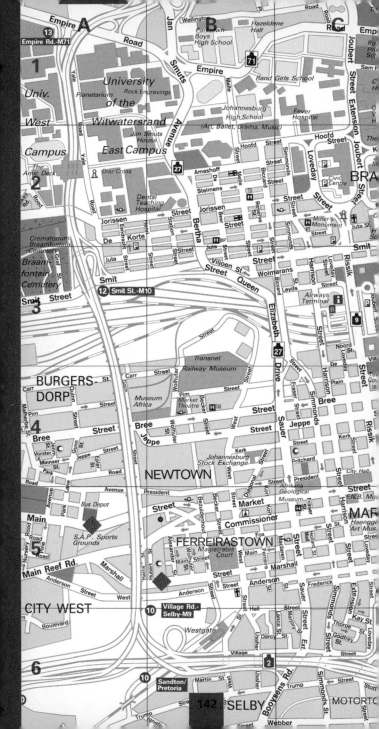